MW01114325

30 Days of Sex Talks
Empowering Your Child with Knowledge of Sexual Intimacy
Ages 12+

Rising Parent Media, LLC
© 2015, 2018 by Rising Parent Media
 Published 2015
Printed in the United States of America

20 19 18 17 16    2 3 4

ISBN: 978-0-9863708-2-3 (paperback)

The paper used in this publication meets the minimum requirements of the American National Standard for Information Sciences–Permanence of Paper for Printed Library Materials, ANSI Z39.48-1992.

www.educateempowerkids.org

# 30 DAYS OF SEX TALKS

FOR AGES
12+

## EMPOWERING YOUR CHILD WITH KNOWLEDGE OF SEXUAL INTIMACY

BY
EDUCATE AND EMPOWER KIDS

**FOR GREAT RESOURCES AND INFORMATION, FOLLOW US:**

Facebook: www.facebook.com/educateempowerkids/
Twitter: @EduEmpowerKids
Pinterest: pinterest.com/educateempower/
Instagram: Eduempowerkids

EDUCATE AND EMPOWER KIDS WOULD LIKE TO ACKNOWLEDGE
THE FOLLOWING PEOPLE WHO CONTRIBUTED TIME,TALENTS,
AND ENERGY TO THIS PUBLICATION:

Dina Alexander, MS
Amanda Scott
Jenny Webb, MA
Caron C. Andrews

Ed Allison
Mary Ann Benson, MSW, LSW
Scott Hounsell
Cliff Park, MBA

**DESIGN AND ILLUSTRATION BY:**
Jera Mehrdad

# 30 DAYS OF SEX TALKS
# TABLE OF CONTENTS

# INTRODUCTION

Sexual intimacy is one of the greatest experiences available to us as human beings. We feel that it is imperative that you are able to clearly express this sentiment to your child. Each of us at Educate and Empower Kids is a parent and like all parents, we feel passionate about providing positive, thought-provoking experiences for our children to learn from. In the world we live in, this is not an easy task.

Our goal is not only to provide you with an opportunity to start conversations about crucial topics, but also to help you create an environment in your home which encourages open discussions about the many other issues which will inevitably come up as you are raising your child. Talking with your child about sex and intimacy is a great way to open the door for other important discussions. After all, this is what makes us human—it's part of what makes the human experience beautiful.

Children in the US spend an average of 7.5 hours consuming media each day (Boyse, RN, 2010). Additionally, according to one study, 42% of children had been exposed to pornography in the past year and of those, 67% were exposed to it *accidentally* (Wolack, et al., 2007). With the amount of sex and violence in almost every medium our kids are watching, we need to ask ourselves what we are doing to counteract all that screen time.

The purpose of this curriculum is to help you as parents establish and grow open and honest communication with your child about sex, intimacy, the dangers of online pornography and your child's view of him or herself. We believe that once you have started these conversations, you will be empowered to talk to your child about anything.

With this program, we've made it simple for you to talk about love, sex, bodies and relationships. You can discuss sex in the context in which it belongs; as a part of a healthy relationship that also includes joy, laughter and the full range of emotion that defines human intimacy.

# GETTINGSTARTED

The curriculum includes a book, glossary and a code to download the topic cards. Each topic is followed by several bullet points. These bullet points contain terms to define and discuss with your child as well as questions or statements designed to inspire conversations between you and your child. We've included definitions, sample dialogue and even some activities to make it simple and to help you get started. It's important to discuss things with your child based on his or her own maturity level; progressing or referring back at your own pace.

You need not be an expert, the hard work has all been done for you. In fact, we feel strongly that leaning on your own personal experiences—both mistakes and successes—is a great way to use life lessons to teach your child. If done properly, these talks will bring you closer to your child than you ever could have imagined. You know and love your child more than anyone, so you decide when and where these discussions take place. In time, you will recognize and enjoy teaching moments in everyday life with your child.

This book works well with the downloadable topic cards (on-line code is available in the back of the book). On the following pages you'll find each topic with its bullet points listed, followed by ideas for further discussion items, questions you may want to ask, and points to consider when talking with your child about that topic. Throughout the book we've also included several suggested scenarios that you could pose to your child to prompt additional thoughts and discussions of specific situations that could arise in his or her life.

Talk about both the emotional and physical aspects of each topic and discuss emotional and physical safety. Be sure to ask your child questions to help draw him or her out. These topics are starting points. If additional or different conversations arise, follow them. This curriculum is designed to be personalized to you and your child. Consistent conversation is the key to suc-cessfully implementing this program. Remember, the goal is not only to present useful information to your child, but to normalize the process of talking to each other about these topics.

We strongly encourage you to read through the suggested topics, bullet points, and ideas in the parent book before talking with your child. Here are a few tips:

- Plan ahead of time but don't create an event. Having a plan or planning ahead of time will remove much of the awkwardness you might feel in talking about these subjects with your child. In not creating an event, you are making the discussions feel more spontaneous, the experience more repeatable and yourself more approachable.

- Consider your individual child's age, developmental stage, and personality in conjunction with each topic, as well as your family's values and individual situation, and adapt the material in order to produce the best discussion.

There are additional resources listed in the back of the book as well as a glossary to help you define the terms used.

# INSTRUCTIONS

# BETHESOURCE

*You* direct the conversations. You love and know your child better than anyone else, so you are the best person to judge what will be most effective: Taking into account personal values, religious beliefs, individual personalities, and family dynamics. If you don't discuss these topics, your child will look for answers from other, less reliable *and sometimes dangerous* sources like: the internet, the media, and other kids.

# FOCUSONINTIMACY

Help your child understand how incredible and uniting sex can be. Don't just focus on the mechanics, spend a significant amount of time talking about the beauty of love and sex, the reality of real relationships and how they are built and maintained. Children are constantly exposed to unhealthy examples of relationships in the media. Many of them are teaching your child lessons about sexuality and interactions between people that are misleading, incomplete, and unhealthy. Real emotional intimacy is rarely portrayed, so it's your job to model positive behavior. You can help your child connect the dots between healthy relationships and healthy sexuality when you model positive ways for your child to like and care for his or her body; to protect, have a positive attitude toward and make favorable choices for that body.

# ANSWERYOURCHILD'SQUESTIONS

If you are embarrassed by your child's curiosity and questions, you imply that there is something shameful about these topics. However, if you answer your child's questions openly and honestly, you demonstrate that sexuality is positive and healthy relationships are something to seek when the time is right. Answer your child's questions honestly and openly and your child will learn that you are available not just for this discussion, but for any discussion. It's okay if you don't have all the answers. Tell your child you will find out for him or her; because it's better that you go searching instead of your child doing so. See the resources at the end of this book and on our resources page at www.educateempowerkids.org for further information on these and other topics.

# BEPOSITIVE

Take the fear and shame out of these discussions. Sex is natural and wondrous and your child should feel nothing but positivity about it from you. If you do feel awkward, stay calm and use matter-of-fact tones and discussion. It's easier than you think- just open your mouth and begin! *It will get easier with every talk you have with your child.* After a couple of talks, he or she will begin to look forward to this time that you are spending together and so will you. Taking the time to talk about these things will reiterate to your child how important he or she is to you. Use experiences from your own life to begin a discussion if it makes you feel more comfortable. We have listed some tough topics here, but they are all discussed in a positive, informative way. Don't worry, we are with you every step of the way!

# NEEDTOKNOW

- This curriculum is not a one-size-fits all. You guide the conversation and lead the discussion according to your unique situation.

- No program can cover all aspects of sexual intimacy perfectly for every individual circumstance. You can empower yourself with the knowledge you gain from this program to share with your child what you feel is the most important.

- This program is meant to be simple! It's presented on cards with bullet points to be straightfoward and create conversations.

# FINALLY

This program is meant to inspire conversations that we hope assist you in fostering an environment where difficult discussions are made easier. The hope is that your child will feel like he or she can talk to you about anything. This program is a great tool that your kids will look forward to! Take advantage of the one on one time that these discussions facilitate to become more comfortable talking with your child.

*It's recommended that you designate with your child and within your home a "safe zone", meaning that during the course of these conversations, your child should feel free and safe to ask any questions and make any comments without judgment or repercussion. Your child should be able to use the term "safe zone" again and again to discuss, confide and consult with you about the tough subjects he or she will be confronted with throughout life.*

*It's highly recommended that, whenever possible, all parenting parties be involved in these discussions.*

**Citations**

*Boyse, RN, K. (2010, August 1). Television (TV) and Children. Retrieved November 13, 2014, from http://www.med.umich.edu/yourchild/topics/tv.htm*

*Wolack, et al. (2007, February 2). Unwanted and Wanted Exposure to Online Pornography in a National Sample of Youth Internet Users. Retrieved November 13, 2014, from http://pediatrics.aappublications.org/content/119/2/247.full*

# LET'S GET STARTED!

# AGES
# 12+

Teenagers generally have more mature and complicated concerns about love, sex, and relationships and how they fit together. Our program is meant to help you approach these subjects and facilitate meaningful dialogue about them, continuing to build on the solid foundation you've established. If you find yourself, like many, broaching these subjects with your kids for the first time at this age, you will find helpful suggestions for how to get your kids engaged in discussing their feelings and experiences. If you feel like your child needs more basic information before discussing the bullet points provided, refer back to the 8-11 age group curriculum.

Throughout these conversations that you'll want to keep up a continuous, non-judgmental dialogue about the topics provided. Remember, your kids feel like adults, so respond as adult-like as possible.

# 1.
# THE PHYSICAL SIDE OF RELATIONSHIPS

- ♛ WHAT ARE SOME DIFFERENT WAYS THAT PEOPLE SHOW AFFECTION?

- ♛ IS THERE A NATURAL PROGRESSION OF AFFECTION IN A RELATIONSHIP?

- ♛ WHO DECIDES THE NEXT STEP IN YOUR RELATIONSHIP?

- ♛ DOES BIOLOGY OR SOCIAL EXPERIENCE DETERMINE HOW PEOPLE FEEL ABOUT SEX?

**AFFECTION:** *A feeling or type of love that exceeds general goodwill.*

## START THE CONVERSATION

Talking about these issues will help teens identify and understand their own ideas and values about physical contact. Share your thoughts and beliefs and perhaps even personal experiences of how you set and enforced your own limits.

Talk about what some of the next steps in a relationship are as it changes from friendship into something else. Be specific according to your beliefs. Ask your teen what other ways people show affection.

Your son or daughter may feel various pressures about taking a relationship to a sexual level: from society, friends, or his or her partner. Help your teen set limits for him or herself now so that the decision need not be made in the heat of the moment at some future point.

Help your teen to come up with a  plan to use if he or she gets into a situation that is becoming too sexual for comfort. Teach your teen ways to VOICE his or her limits to their partner—to say what he/she needs or wants in a relationship! Make this very specific so that your teen won't get caught off guard in the middle of a situation with another person.

Discuss your thoughts and ask for your teen's ideas on where societal concepts of sex come from. For example, a guy is often considered a "stud" for having multiple sex partners while a girl is considered promiscuous or slutty. Discuss all aspects of nature versus nurture and whether or not both are significant factors in people's ideas about sex.

# ADDITIONAL QUESTIONS TO CONSIDER

How do you know if you're ready to kiss someone?

How do you know if someone is ready to kiss you?

Where is the line between showing physical affection and turning that affection sexual?

Which of the following shows affection? Active listening, a gentle touch on the arm, smiling at each other, and/or maintaining eye contact? What other things show affection?

If you get into a situation that is becoming too sexual for your comfort, what will you do and say?

What will be your exit plan in that situation?

Do societal concepts of sex come from biology?

Are boys and girls born with certain inherent sexual urges and feelings?

Are girls and boys socialized about sex in different ways?

How do your family ideals about sex fit into your concept of sex?

How does peer pressure factor into your concept of sex?

## SAMPLE SCENARIO

Pose the following scenario to your teen to enhance the discussion and bring the subject into a real-life context: You and your girlfriend have been getting physically closer the past few weeks with more intense kissing. You know you're on the edge of becoming sexually active with her. You've already decided how you feel about having sex—what circumstances will have to be in place and you do/don't want. Even so, you don't feel sure of what you want with her. Your girlfriend clearly feels sure about how she wants to proceed/not proceed. How will you decide individually and as a couple what to do? What will you say to begin that conversation? Whose needs and wishes should prevail? How can you say "no"?

# 2.
# SEX

- 👑 WHAT IS SEX?

- 👑 WHAT "COUNTS" AS SEX?

- 👑 WHAT TYPES OF SEX ARE THERE?

📖 **INTERCOURSE:** *Sexual activity, also known as coitus or copulation, which is most commonly understood to refer to the insertion of the penis into the vagina (vaginal sex). It should be noted that there are a wide range of various sexual activities and the boundaries of what constitutes sexual intercourse are still under debate.*

# START THE CONVERSATION

You may think that you don't need to discuss this level of specifics with your kids, but the reality is that sexually active teens are actively trying every kind of sex. Since your kids are going to hear things about it, you need to talk with them about how they define it. Initiating this conversation helps you to be the source of information.

Ask your kids what they define as sex. Various kinds of sex that were probably not discussed when you were a teenager are now part of everyday talk, so explain the types. Please see the glossary for definitions of vaginal sex, anal sex, and oral sex, as well as orgasm. This describes the mechanics; steer the conversation towards emotions, acceptability of these acts, and morality according to your values. You can be a powerful influence on how your teenagers feel about various forms of sexual contact and their personal decisions about them.

# ADDITIONAL QUESTIONS TO CONSIDER

Is it sex if there is mutual sexual contact?

Is sex anything that results in an orgasm?

Is it sex if your sex organs are touching?

Is it sex if your clothes are on?

# 3.
# EMOTIONAL INTIMACY

- THE BEST SEX HAS STRONG EMOTIONAL CONNECTION

- DO YOU NEED EMOTIONAL INTIMACY TO HAVE SEX?

- IS IT OKAY TO HAVE SEX FOR PURELY PHYSICAL SATISFACTION?

- CAN YOU HAVE TRUE INTIMACY WITHOUT A PHYSICAL RELATIONSHIP?

## START THE CONVERSATION

Popular culture tends to portray sex as purely physical rather than based on a relationship. The point of this topic is to connect emotions and relationships with sex for your kids.

Emotional intimacy includes sharing feelings, ideas, dreams, experiences, and trust with another person. It's respecting each other's differences and celebrating each other's uniqueness. It's caring for the other person as much as you care for yourself, or more, and wanting what is best for that person.

Explain that physical sensations are wonderful in themselves, but when combined with a deep emotional connection, the experience is much more than the physical aspect. Guide the conversation according to your beliefs and values, but talk about why people may have sex for only physical satisfaction. Talk about under what circumstances could this be acceptable, if ever.

Many people confuse sex with true closeness or intimacy, but they can be two separate things, depending on the emotions involved.

**INTIMACY:** *An aspect of relationships that is dependent upon trust and that can be expressed both verbally and non-verbally. Emotional intimacy displays a degree of closeness that exceeds that normally experienced in common relational interactions.*

# ADDITIONAL QUESTIONS TO CONSIDER

Why does a strong emotional connection with your partner enhance sexual experiences?

How do you think you want to feel about a person with whom you will have sex?

How important is trust in a healthy sexual relationship?

How important is respect in a healthy sexual relationship?

How important is love in a healthy sexual relationship?

Is it okay to have sex for physical satisfaction only?

Can two people be truly intimate without having a sexual relationship?

Why does the media rarely portray sex as needing true intimacy?

# 4.
# SEX MEANS DIFFERENT THINGS TO BOYS AND GIRLS

- ♛ WHAT DOES SEX MEAN TO YOU?

- ♛ IS IT A MYTH THAT BOYS ONLY WANT TO HAVE SEX FOR PHYSICAL GRATIFICATION?

- ● MANY PEOPLE, ESPECIALLY FEMALES, EQUATE HAVING SEX WITH BEING LOVED

**PERCEPTION:** *A way of regarding, understanding, or interpreting something; a mental impression.*

## START THE CONVERSATION

Due to differences in how boys and girls or men and women are socialized into their view sex, it's important that the couple talk about it before engaging in it. Teach your kids that open and honest communication will not lessen the romance; rather, it will enhance the relationship if each person understands the other's thoughts and feelings.

Remember that you are steering the conversation and can approach it according to your opinions and values.

## ADDITIONAL QUESTIONS TO CONSIDER

Sex means different things to boys and girls. How does this affect their social behavior and actions?

Do boys want emotional closeness in sex?

If your boyfriend or girlfriend wants to have sex with you, does that mean they love you?

Can you love someone romantically without it leading to sex?

How would you feel about a girl who only has sex for physical reasons?

How would you feel about a boy who only has sex for physical reasons?

If you have the desire to have sex with a boyfriend or girlfriend, does that mean you love them?

14

# 5.
# POSITIVE ASPECTS OF SEX

- IT FOSTERS EMOTIONAL BONDING/CLOSENESS/UNITY

- IT'S FUN

- IT CAN BE A CONNECTION ON THE MOST HUMAN/INTIMATE LEVEL POSSIBLE

- IT FEELS AWESOME

**HEALTHY SEXUALITY:** *Having the ability to express one's sexuality in ways that contribute positively to one's own self-esteem and relationships. Healthy sexuality includes approaching sexual relationships and interactions with mutual agreement and dignity. It necessarily includes mutual respect and a lack of fear, shame, or guilt, and never includes coercion or violence.*

## START THE CONVERSATION

There are a lot of negative connotations about sex all around us--because there is a negative side to it. The tragic side of sex can be found in pornography, child molestation, rape, sexual abuse, and the rape culture that is becoming more prevalent, all of which are addressed in upcoming topics. However, you can counteract those influences with your kids. Since teenagers are bombarded daily with the negative side of sex, teach them that there is a good, healthy, pleasurable, and respectful side of sex.

The focus and scope of this discussion should be driven by your values and opinions and your communication style with your kids.

Talk with your teens about the unifying and bonding feelings that sex between loving, committed partners can create. Explain that sex is supposed to be pleasurable and satisfying under the right circumstances. Teach your teenager that it's an amazing, fantastic thing to create life when you're emotionally and financially ready. You could talk about the planning process and anticipation of when you were pregnant or preparing to welcome a baby into your home.

Emphasize that a healthy outcome of connecting physically is connecting emotionally on a very intimate and human level. Intense and vulnerable feelings naturally flow from healthy sex between people who care about one another. This is the amazing and bonding aspect that makes sex very special and personal to the couple. Sex is meant to unify two people in this way; it is meant to be good.

## ADDITIONAL QUESTIONS TO CONSIDER

What positive things have you heard about sex?

What do you think would make it the most positive experience it could be?

Does it include emotional closeness?

Does it include chemistry between you and the other person?

Does it include trust?

Can you have a positive experience with hook-up sex?

Are the physical feelings associated with sex as pleasurable as the emotional?

# 6.
# PHYSICAL RESPONSES TO SEX

- ♛ WHAT HAPPENS WHEN A MALE IS SEXUALLY AROUSED?

- ♛ WHAT HAPPENS WHEN A FEMALE IS SEXUALLY AROUSED?

- 💬 PHYSICAL RESPONSES TO SEX ARE INDIVIDUAL

# START THE CONVERSATION

Your personal comfort level and dynamics with your teenager will naturally dictate how you approach this topic. Guide this conversation according to your ideas and beliefs about the nature of sex. Our point in including this topic is to help you educate your kids about positive physical reactions to sex and how wonderful they can be under the right circumstances, and about possible negative physical reactions. Knowing a range of responses that are considered anywhere from healthy to problematic can help your kids to understand themselves, their future partner, and healthy sexuality. Be sure to include your values and family expectations into the questions.

According to your comfort level, explain the physical progression of female arousal (see glossary for definition). When a female is aroused, the nipples and external genitals, including the labia and clitoris (see glossary for definitions), become engorged. There is vaginal lubrication and secretions, which aid in physically comfortable intercourse. The vagina enlarges with arousal.

Discuss the physical progression of male arousal. When stimulated, blood flow to the penis increases, causing an erection (see glossary for definition). During this process, the skin of the scrotum (see glossary) tightens and the testicles (see glossary) are pulled in close to the body. The head of the penis typically enlarges with the influx of blood. Prior to ejaculation (see glossary), some fluid may be released from the tip of the penis. At the climax of sexual excitement, ejaculation occurs.

📖 **AROUSAL:** *The physical and emotional response to sexual desire during or in anticipation of sexual activity.*

Not all male erections are due to sexual arousal. Talk about spontaneous erections (see glossary), which can occur when awake or asleep for physiological, non-sexual reasons.

You may want to discuss specific sexual problems that can occur. Some of them are priapism (see glossary), which is a male's prolonged erection; vaginismus (see glossary), which is the inability to penetrate vaginally; female vaginal dryness, which can make intercourse uncomfortable or painful; and erectile dysfunction, which is the male's inability to achieve an erection or problems keeping one.

It's important to note that the growing rate of erectile dysfunction in the male population is linked to prolonged exposure to and use of pornography (Voon, et. al., 2014). You may want to talk about this with your kids both now and when you discuss Pornography (topic #17).

# ADDITIONAL QUESTIONS TO CONSIDER

Is it okay for a girl or for a boy to be aroused?

Why is sexual arousal so powerful?

Should sexual arousal be controlled or is it okay to always act on it if it's a natural force?

Can you be aroused without having a sexual experience?

What can you do when you are aroused but don't want to follow through on those feelings?

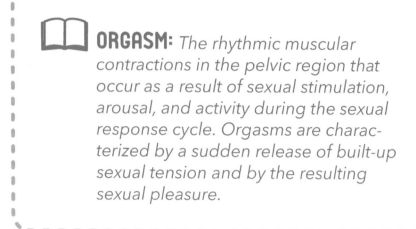

**ORGASM:** *The rhythmic muscular contractions in the pelvic region that occur as a result of sexual stimulation, arousal, and activity during the sexual response cycle. Orgasms are characterized by a sudden release of built-up sexual tension and by the resulting sexual pleasure.*

## START THE CONVERSATION

Orgasm is a natural part of sex. It's a huge topic of conversation and a focal point in pornography, which has filtered down through the mainstream, making its importance inflated and exaggerated. It's important for teenagers to understand what it is, what it's for, and how its presence or absence can affect an intimate sexual relationship. If you are comfortable, discuss with your teen that there are different ways of achieving an orgasm, and the potential for multiple orgasms.

Female orgasm is frequently achieved as a result of the physical sexual stimulation of the clitoris (see glossary) and results in a release of the buildup of sexual tension and excitement through involuntary spasms of the pelvic area and vagina (see glossary). It is accompanied by a general euphoric and intensely pleasurable physical sensation and can include spontaneous vocalizations.

# 7.
# ORGASM

- WHAT IS AN ORGASM?

- DO YOU NEED TO HAVE AN ORGASM FOR SEX TO BE FULFILLING?

- MEN AND WOMEN ACHIEVE ORGASM DIFFERENTLY

For centuries, female pleasure and female orgasm have not been considered important or even acceptable. It is very important to teach your daughter that her sexual experience is just as important as her partner's. Talk to your daughter about how she can achieve orgasm. Discuss clitoral stimulation and other erogenous zones. It is also important to teach your sons that a good partner helps his partner achieve orgasm.

Males generally reach orgasm through physical sexual stimulation of the penis, beginning with getting an erection (see glossary). At the point of climax, sexual tension and excitement typically culminate in ejaculation (see glossary) and involuntary spasms in the pelvic area. As with female orgasm, it is accompanied by a general euphoric and intensely pleasurable physical sensation and can include spontaneous vocalizations.

Discuss nocturnal emissions (see glossary), which are orgasms in either males or females that occur spontaneously during sleep. A common expression for them in males is "wet dreams."

Have a discussion about epididymal hypertension (see glossary), commonly called "blue balls," which occurs when fluid temporarily overfills the testicles because of prolonged and unfulfilled sexual arousal. It can cause pain or discomfort in the testicles. Are you obligated to complete a sexual act once begun in order to avoid his discomfort? The absolute, irrevocable answer to this is no.

Finally, it is critical to teach your kids that it is okay to express their sexual needs to their partner. This seems to be more difficult for women, as many are not taught that their sexual needs are important.

# ADDITIONAL QUESTIONS TO CONSIDER

How does orgasm differ for males and females?

Is achieving an orgasm imperative for a man?

Is achieving an orgasm imperative for a woman?

Do you think that the other aspects of sex are just as important, or is having an orgasm the most important factor?

If orgasm is not achieved, is it something to feel bad about?

Do most couple's orgasms happen at the same time (as portrayed in TV and movies)?

Are you obligated to complete a sexual act once begun in order to avoid his discomfort? (The absolute, irrevocable answer to this is no.)

Do you have any questions?

# 8.
# RELATIONSHIP BOUNDARIES

- AT WHAT AGE IS IT OKAY TO HAVE SEX?

- AT WHAT POINT IN A RELATIONSHIP IS IT OKAY TO HAVE SEX?

- IS IT OKAY TO STOP ONCE YOU'VE STARTED?

- SHOULD YOU BE IN A COMMITTED RELATIONSHIP BEFORE HAVING SEX?

**BOUNDARIES:** *The personal limits or guidelines that an individual forms in order to clearly identify what are reasonable and safe behaviors for others to engage in around him or her.*

## START THE CONVERSATION

This discussion continues some of the points from the Physical Side of Relationships discussion (topic #1). Encourage your kids to make a decision about their limits before they are in a sexual situation. Explain and make sure your teens understand that they never have to have sex if they don't want to. The objective here is for your teens to come to know on their own that it's okay to stop once started, and that it's okay to not start in the first place. Express your feelings about sex before marriage, sex in a committed relationship, and casual sex. You can help guide your kids to make their decisions.

## ADDITIONAL QUESTIONS TO CONSIDER

Is it appropriate to act on physical urges if both are in agreement?

How do age and length of relationship affect physical expectations?

What is a committed relationship?

Is a committed relationship based on feelings?

Can a committed relationship happen within a week?

Should a committed relationship be in place before having sex with the person?

How can you know your own limits?

How can you learn to know yourself and your inner voice?

What other factors figure into when it's okay to have sex?

If your partner is ready for sex but you're not sure, is it okay to put a limit on physical contact?

What role does self-respect play in setting your boundaries?

Is it okay to have different boundaries than your friends do?

## SAMPLE SCENARIO

Pose the following scenario to your teen to enhance the discussion and bring the subject into a real-life context: Your best friend comes to you for advice on what to do with a person they're wildly attracted to and who has made it clear they'd be up for a sexual hook-up. You have definite opinions about being in favor of or against casual hook-up sex with someone you're physically attracted to but have no relationship with. What will you say to your friend? What kinds of questions could you ask him/her to help him/her come to a decision that's right for him/her?

# 9.
# THE
# FIRST
# TIME

- ♛ WHAT ARE YOUR EXPECTATIONS FOR YOUR FIRST TIME?

- ♛ HOW WILL YOU FEEL/REACT IF IT'S DIFFERENT?

- ♛ HOW WILL YOU KNOW YOU ARE READY?

# START THE CONVERSATION

Reiterate your family values and personal thoughts on when it is appropriate to have sex for the first time. Be sure to bring in your family's religious views, if applicable. Talk about the emotional impact of a sexual relationship. Discuss that some girls/women experience some slight pain (or a lot of pain) with their first intercourse due to tightening of vaginal muscles or the stretching or breaking of the hymen (see glossary).

Have a discussion about how having sex changes a relationship. Help your teen develop a sense of sex being a special bond between two people. Emphasize that they can decide beforehand the circumstances they will require for their first time.

Talk about premature ejaculation (see glossary) and how it can impact a sexual experience physically and emotionally. Discuss the myth that a girl can't get pregnant the first time and the importance of birth control. More information on birth control can be found under Birth Control (topic #30).

**VIRGIN:** *A male or female who has never engaged in sexual intercourse.*

# ADDITIONAL QUESTIONS TO CONSIDER

Is it okay to have sex for the first time if you are in love and in a committed relationship?

When you imagine your ideal first time, are you married?

Is the ideal situation being in a solid, committed relationship?

Is the ideal situation being with a sexy stranger with whom sparks are flying?

Can a relationship ever go back to what it was before having sex?

What do you think might be some negative changes in a relationship once you've started having sex?

What do you think might be some positive changes in a relationship once you've started having sex?

What if after your first time you don't like it? Will it always be that way? How should you talk about it with your partner?

# 10.
# CONSENT

- HOW DO YOU KNOW HE OR SHE REALLY MEANS YES?

- WHAT IS RAPE?

- IS IT OKAY TO STOP ONCE YOU'VE STARTED?

- WHAT IS RAPE CULTURE?

**CONSENT:** *Clear agreement or permission to permit something or to do something. Consent must be given freely, without force or intimidation, and while the person is fully conscious and cognizant of their present situation.*

# START THE CONVERSATION

It's crucial that your teens understand what constitutes consent when it comes to sex, both for themselves and for others, so that they will know when "yes" really means "yes."

There's an old notion (often portrayed in porn) that when a woman says no, she really means yes. Discuss this and possible reasons for it with your teens. If you find that your kids have bought into the notion that "no" really means "yes," emphatically set them straight.

Having sex with someone without their consent is forcible or coerced rape. Date rape doesn't just happen on college campuses, so talk with your kids about this type of rape as well. Discuss how to stay safe in various situations. Come up with a plan!

Being slapped, pinched, grabbed, or touched in any way that's not wanted or uncomfortable is to be touched without your consent. If it's unwanted, it needs to stop. Emphasize that your kids should expect to be treated with respect and dignity everywhere.

If there is anyone who touches your teens in a way that they don't consent to, it needs to be immediately stopped so that it doesn't progress. This kind of touching can start with a "test touch," such as a touch to the arm or a hug, then progress more and more to the point that it is uncomfortable and unwanted.

Tell your teenagers that even if they liked hugging or other physical contact with someone before, they can stop it if it becomes uncomfortable or more than they want.

Point out the types of things that make up rape culture, such as blaming the victim, making jokes about rape, gender violence in movies, assuming that only promiscuous women—and never men—get raped, and tolerance of sexual harassment. An informative resource on rape culture is available at: http://www.marshall.edu/wcenter/sexual-assault/rape-culture/ Consent is also discussed in Unwanted Sexual Attention (topic #23).

An excellent resource for helping to teach your kids about consent throughout childhood, adolescence, and young adulthood can be found in our free downloadable lesson, "Talking to Your Kids About Consent." This is also in Unwanted Sexual Attention (topic #23). Please see the glossary for definitions of test touch, rape, rape culture, and sexual harassment.

# ADDITIONAL QUESTIONS TO CONSIDER

How does good communication relate to determining what your partner truly wants?

How do trust and emotional sensitivity relate to determining what your partner truly wants?

If a person does not respect another's "no," when does it become harassment?

What does it mean to be violated?

If a person is using drugs or alcohol, how does that affect his or her ability to give true consent?

What else could make it hard to give true consent?

What plan can you have if you find yourself in a situation where you are not longer comfortable?

# SAMPLE SCENARIO

Pose the following scenario to your teen to enhance the discussion and bring the subject into a real-life context: You are at a party and you've had two beers. You don't normally drink and you're feeling a bit lightheaded. Everything seems silly. You're flirting back and forth with a guy/girl you know from math class but have never really noticed before. You feel silly and giddy, and he/she suddenly seems like the greatest person in the room. He/she has also had a few drinks, and starts making sexual overtures toward you. You've never thought of him/her like that before, but you feel so tipsy that sex with him/her seems like a good idea. You find a secluded spot together and have sex.

**Questions:**

Have you truly given consent?

Has he/she?

Do you think this would play out differently if one or both of you weren't impaired?

# SURVEY 1 **12+**

**Please reflect on your discussions with your child up to this point and answer the following questions.**

1. Select the topic that has provided the best discussion with your child thus far.

   1. The Physical Side of Relationships
   2. Sex
   3. Emotional Intimacy
   4. Sex Means Different Things to Boys and Girls
   5. Positive Aspects of Sex
   6. Physical Responses to Sex
   7. Orgasm
   8. Relationship Boundaries
   9. The First Time
   10. Consent

2. Referring to question 1, please describe what made this your best discussion.

   _____

   _____

3. Referring to question 1, were there things that you did during your discussion that were different from other discussions? If so, what were they and can you replicate them?

   _____

   _____

4. What has your child said that surprised you during your first 10 discussions?

_____

_____


5. If you have any additional comments, please write them here:

_____

_____


**If you scan the code below, you can take this survey online. This will help us improve our curriculum and create new resources for parents.**

# 11.
# CREATING A HEALTHY RELATIONSHIP

- 💬 LEARNING TO COMMUNICATE

- 💬 CULTIVATING RESPECT AND DIGNITY

- 💬 DEVELOPING HEALTHY IDEAS OF INTIMACY

- 👑 WHAT DO YOU THINK CONSTITUTES A HEALTHY RELATIONSHIP?

📖 **INTIMACY:** *Generally a feeling or form of significant closeness. There are four types of intimacy: physical intimacy (sensual proximity or touching), emotional intimacy (close connection resulting from trust and love), cognitive or intellectual intimacy (resulting from honest exchange of thoughts and ideas), and experiential intimacy (a connection that occurs while acting together). Emotional and physical intimacy are often associated with sexual relationships, while intellectual and experiential intimacy are not.*

## START THE CONVERSATION:

Healthy relationships in all areas of our lives are important to our happiness and sense of well-being. They're also the basis of positive, healthy sexual experiences when your teen is ready. The hypersexualized and porn-influenced culture that kids are steeped in doesn't teach about true intimacy, emotions, or healthy relationships. Guide this discussion with your opinions, beliefs, and values in mind.

Discuss your vision and hope for the kind of committed relationship your children will have when the time is right. Point out examples of healthy relationships in your teen's life.

Teach your teens that both people in a relationship deserve respect and dignity, and no two people are going to agree 100% of the time. You can disagree without destroying the relationship or each other emotionally. Explain that this is the time your teenagers are learning about relationships with the hope of learning what true intimacy is. Part of this is learning to disagree, and that disagreements are okay. Talk about what is appropriate etiquette when fighting, such as not calling names and not bringing up past arguments.

Power struggles within a relationship can make one person feel inferior to the other. Talk with your teens about how power struggles can be diminished when each person has a healthy sense of self as well as respect for him or herself and the other.

## ADDITIONAL QUESTIONS TO CONSIDER

What kind of behaviors, language, and actions does a healthy relationship include?

How does it feel when you're in a healthy relationship?

Is there room to be individuals as well as a couple?

How will you let your partner know how you're feeling?

How will you tell them what you want and what you don't want? How can you be clear in your communication?

How can you express your opinion or stance without ridiculing the other person?

How does the use of sweeping terms like "always" and "never" inflame the disagreement?

How can you enhance or encourage another person's dignity?

What could you do to bring balance back to a relationship that has become a power struggle?

What can each person do to acknowledge the other's importance and feelings without trivializing their own?

How will this help establish or restore healthy intimacy in the relationship?

# SAMPLE SCENARIO

Pose the following scenario to your teen to enhance the discussion and bring the subject into a real-life context: You and a classmate of the opposite sex are becoming good friends. He/she has been teasing you about a birthmark you have on your arm that you initially joked about. Lately, though, his/her comments and jokes are making you uncomfortable, self-conscious, and mad. How will you handle this? Will you hope he/she takes a hint when you stop laughing along with him/her? Will you say something to him/her directly the next time it happens? Will you snap at him/her and walk away?

# 12.
# ABUSIVE
# RELATIONSHIPS

- ABUSE CAN BE EMOTIONAL, MENTAL, PHYSICAL, AND/OR SEXUAL

- WHY ARE SOME PEOPLE ABUSIVE TO OTHERS?

- HOW DO YOU STOP ABUSE?

# START THE CONVERSATION

The United States Department of Justice defines domestic violence as "a pattern of abusive behavior in any relationship that is used by one partner to gain or maintain power and control over another intimate partner. Domestic violence can be physical, sexual, emotional, economic, or psychological actions or threats of actions that influence another person. This includes any behaviors that intimidate, manipulate, humiliate, isolate, frighten, terrorize, coerce, threaten, blame, hurt, injure, or wound someone."

Abuse can be anything from persistent disrespect all the way to violence. Please see the glossary for more information about abuse. This is a great time to talk about why it's so important for your kids to develop their interests and talents, build their sense of self-worth, and treat themselves kindly. Because the stronger they are in these areas, the less likely they will be vulnerable to being abused. More information can be found in Liking Yourself (topic #14).

**DOMESTIC ABUSE/ DOMESTIC VIOLENCE:** *A pattern of abusive behavior in any relationship that is used by one partner to gain or maintain power and control over another intimate partner. It can be physical, sexual, emotional, economic, or psychological actions or threats of actions that influence another person. (DOJ definition)*

Communicate to your teenager that it's not okay to call names. It's not okay for anyone to speak to you in a way you don't like. It's not okay for anyone to put their hands on you in a way you don't like. Repeated exposure to this kind of treatment desensitizes the victim to it, and because of that, he or she may not easily identify escalated abuse for what it is.

It's very important to understand that abusers do not start out abusing right away, and often can be wonderful and charming and have great qualities, if they didn't they would not be in a relationship. Teach your teen to trust his/her gut instinct. If something does not feel right trust it, don't wait for something bad to happen.

Talk about what a person can do to get out of an abusive relationship and stop the cycle. Telling others about the abuse is a key step. It can be hard to identify it in boyfriend/girlfriend relationships because of the emotions involved. Common scenarios and situations are identified at http://www.webmd.com/a-to-z-guides/teen-relationship-abuse-topic-overview. Emphasize that there are people your teen can talk to, such as trained teachers and counselors at school, and you as their parents. There are also help centers and hotlines.

If you or your teen believes he/she is a victim of abuse, please get help. A wealth of in-depth information and help can be found in these great resources:

http://www.justice.gov/ovw/domestic-violence

http://www.thehotline.org/

# ADDITIONAL QUESTIONS TO CONSIDER

What do you think constitutes an abusive relationship?

What kind of behaviors, language, and actions
does it include?

How do you think it feels when you're in an abusive relationship?

Why would a person be abusive to another?

Could an abusive person have been abused themselves?

Can a person who has been abused as a child grow up to have
healthy relationships?

How can you identify abusive people and situations?

# 13.
# SELF-WORTH AND SEX

- HOW DOES SELF-WORTH AFFECT YOUR DECISIONS ABOUT INTIMACY?

- A PERSON WHO LOVES AND RESPECTS THEMSELVES WILL NOT DEMEAN OTHERS

- WILL SEX EMPOWER OR DIMINISH YOU?

**SELF-ESTEEM/SELF-WORTH:**
*An individual's overall emotional evaluation of their own worth. Self-esteem is both a judgment of the self and an attitude toward the self. More generally, the term is used to describe a confidence in one's own value or abilities.*

## START THE CONVERSATION

The foundation for a healthy sexuality comes from our own feelings about ourselves and others. Those feelings are integral to how we relate to others and they impact our desires, decisions, and actions toward relationships, intimacy, and sex.

Many people equate sex with love, thinking that if someone wants to have sex with them, that person must love them or want a relationship with them. In this way, people sometimes have sex as a way to boost their sense of self-worth. Talk about ways people build their self-worth and self-esteem.

Sex can be positive and connecting; it can also be damaging and cheapening. Tell your kids that they have a lot of power over how their sexual experiences will be. Talk again about Emotional Intimacy (topic #3).

# ADDITIONAL QUESTIONS TO CONSIDER

Is feeling sexy and wanted a valid means of feeling good about yourself?

Is self-worth built by accomplishing goals?

Are self-esteem and self-worth built by taking care of yourself emotionally and physically?

Are they built by believing that you are worthy of respect and dignity simply for being a human being?

How might a person who feels good about themselves approach sex differently from someone who does not?

If you feel good about yourself, how will you treat someone else?

If you feel bad about yourself, how will you treat another?

Is it better to be alone than to be with someone who pressures you?

How do you know if you really want sex or if you're just going along with it?

Should you act in the moment or make a decision about having sex ahead of time?

How can you live without regrets?

# 14.
# LIKING YOURSELF

- YOU ARE ENTITLED TO GREAT RELATIONSHIPS

- YOU CAN MAKE GREAT DECISIONS

- YOU ARE ENTITLED TO GENUINE INTIMACY

# START THE CONVERSATION

It's important that your kids recognize and acknowledge what's great about them. Everyone has special talents, interests, mannerisms, and characteristics that make them the unique person they are. Appreciating what's great about yourself is the basis of liking yourself. When you like yourself, you know that you're entitled to great relationships and genuine intimacy and that you can make great decisions. Having a strong foundation of liking themselves will pave the way to this for your kids.

Help your kids celebrate who they are and encourage the special qualities you see in them by talking about your impression of them. Give specific examples of things they've done or said that you admire or thought were impressive. Sometimes it's hard for a kid to see those things, so point them out to them: tell your child five to fifty things that are awesome about them. You can even continue to do this throughout their lives. In this way you can be a mirror for them to help show them the fantastic people they are!

Then tell your teenagers that no one expects them to be perfect: we all make mistakes, but they are destined for greatness. Let your teens know that what they do or don't do sexually is

📖 **POSITIVE SELF-TALK:** *Anything said to oneself for encouragement or motivation, such as phrases or mantras; also, one's ongoing internal conversation with oneself, like a running commentary, which influences how one feels and behaves.*

not the sum total of who they are. It's not a reflection on their self-worth. Discuss self-worth: what it is, where it comes from, and how it affects relationships. Please see the glossary for more information.

Talk to your teens about the option of waiting to have sex. Emphasize that you can't have great sex without knowing how to have great intimacy. But also remind your kids that if they have been sexually active and regret it, it should not overshadow their self-worth or define who they are. Reinforce that your kids are capable of making good decisions for themselves.

# ADDITIONAL QUESTIONS TO CONSIDER

What do you like about yourself?

What are some of your strengths?

How is sex linked with liking yourself?

Do you think differently of friends who have had sex versus friends who have not?

Will you think more or less about yourself after becoming sexually active? Or will you feel the same about yourself?

What are the healthy emotional and intellectual elements a person should have before having sex?

Do you have all of those healthy elements?

# SAMPLE SCENARIO

Pose the following scenario to your teen to enhance the discussion and bring the subject into a real-life context: There's a popular group of kids at school that is known for having parties with lots of alcohol and casual sex. Part of you is secretly a little in awe of them and sometimes you imagine being a part of the group. Now you've been invited to one of these parties. How will you decide what to do? What questions could you ask yourself to discover what draws you to this group? How will you feel about yourself if you go? How will you feel about yourself if you go and drink and possibly have sex under those circumstances?

# 15.
# BODY IMAGE AND SEX

- ♛ HOW DOES BODY IMAGE AFFECT OUR INHERENT SENSE OF VALUE?

- ♛ HOW DO YOU FEEL ABOUT THE WAY YOU LOOK?

- ♛ DO YOU CREATE RELATIONSHIPS BASED ON PEOPLE'S LOOKS?

- ♛ WILL YOUR BODY IMAGE AFFECT YOUR SEX LIFE?

**BODY IMAGE:** *An individual's feelings regarding their own physical attractiveness and sexuality. These feelings and opinions are often influenced by other people and media sources.*

# START THE CONVERSATION

Body image is about more than just how your teen thinks his or her body looks; it's about how those beliefs impact your teen's thoughts and feelings about themselves. It's about the desire to be attractive and desirable to others. It's entwined with self-worth. It impacts relationships with others too. Body image is an important topic that warrants in-depth discussion.

Recap with your teens the previous topic, Liking Yourself (topic #14). Developing healthy body image improves self-esteem. How your teenagers feel about their body affects how they feel about themselves, which is a key indicator of what kind of relationships/friendships they make. Share your feelings about your body and struggles you may have had about it.

There's a lot of pressure on teenagers about appearance. What can you do to help if your child is struggling with a negative body image? Discuss the many amazing and awesome things everyone's body can do, like healing itself and allowing us to see, hear, taste, feel, run, cry, dance, laugh, and generally experience the world. If your kids can learn to appreciate these things, they are much more likely to develop a healthy body image. If your teen feels like he or she wants to improve, talk about healthy eating, exercise, getting enough sleep, and drinking enough water.

Our culture is enormously focused on looks and appearance. Even though we know that people's character and "inner beauty" are more important, we can't help but be influenced by the media's obsession with looks.

Discuss media influences and how narrow ideas of beauty affect all people. Discuss how computer images show impossible standards that no one looks like, even the people in the pictures or films. We'll be talking about this in the next topic, Being Media Savvy (topic #16).

# ADDITIONAL QUESTIONS TO CONSIDER

How does the way you view your body affect the way you feel about yourself as a whole?

In what ways do you take care of your body and keep it healthy?

What do like best about the way you look?

Are there things about your appearance you wish you could change?

How does your body contribute to who you are as a person?

When you first meet someone, do their looks affect how you think of them?

How do others' opinions affect your body image? Is it negative or positive?

How can you prevent other's opinions from influencing what you think about yourself?

Would you pursue a relationship or friendship with someone you like but who is not "beautiful" or "handsome?"

Does a person have to look like someone on TV for others to be attracted to him/her?

Besides looks, what are some other things that attract us to other people?

Why do some people seek out sexual attention?

How would your body image affect your ability to enjoy sex?

Why do some people think they should avoid sex if they think they are too fat, too thin, or have other reservations about the way they look?

**MEDIA LITERACY:** *The ability to study, understand, and create messages in various media such as books, social media posts, and photos, movies, games, music, news stories, online ads, blog posts, school essays, etc. A critical approach to media focuses on analyzing and evaluating the media in terms of its intended audience, message, and creator, as well as noting the various ways in which facts are manipulated, spun, or even discarded in order to promote a particular reaction or interpretation.*

## START THE CONVERSATION

The media—internet, books, magazines, TV, movies, music—is full of powerful sexual messages that try to convince us that a person's sexiness is one of their most, if not the most, important attributes. Encourage your kids to think critically about the images they see and the messages that are being relayed.

Point out that many media images are trying to sell something and do not represent reality. Advertisers and others use sex because it's a powerful tool in grabbing people's attention for whatever purpose they have. People come in all shapes and sizes because we're not meant to all be the same or fall into a single, narrow definition of beauty.

Emphasize that the people we see in media images frequently don't really look like that because they've been touched up by computer or photoshopped.

# 16.
# BEING MEDIA SAVVY

- WHAT DOES THE MEDIA TEACH US ABOUT SEX AND RELATIONSHIPS?

- HOW CAN YOU CREATE YOUR OWN IDEAS ABOUT SEX AND RELATIONSHIPS SEPARATE FROM A CULTURE OF POWERFUL MEDIA MESSAGES?

- LEARN TO DECONSTRUCT MEDIA: TO BREAK DOWN AN AD, MOVIE COMMERCIAL, SONG, OR OTHER MEDIA INTO PIECES TO SEE WHAT THE REAL MESSAGE IS

Consider with your kids how many hours a week we as a family are spending on media. Teach your teens to deconstruct images by understanding who the audience for media images is, what they're trying to communicate or sell, and why those particular people were used for the images. Teach your teenagers that advertisers have a vested interest in you feeling bad about yourself and therefore buying their products and "miracle" remedies.

## ADDITIONAL QUESTIONS TO CONSIDER

How does the media portray beauty?

How does the media portray sexual relationships?

How can you be true to yourself in a culture of powerful media messages?

Does the media reflect the general attitudes about sex and relationships you see in your daily life?

Do your personal values and attitudes reflect what you see in popular books, movies, or TV? Why is it important to form your own ideas without simply following the messages in pop culture?

What do you think beauty is?

How do you feel about the relationships and interactions you see portrayed in the media?

How many hours a week are we as a family spending on media?

Are we unplugging enough to have meaningful relationships?

# ACTIVITY

Teach your teens to deconstruct images--this is a skill that everyone should practice, not just kids. With your kids, look at an ad in a magazine, online, or anywhere. This same activity can be done with movies, news, and even social media feeds!

Answer the following questions:

What is the overall message?

Why was this ad made?

What did they use to sell this product? (certain objects, words, font styles, Photoshop)

How does this advertisement make you feel?

What is the underlying or hidden message?

What methods were used in this ad to get our attention?

What do the creators want us to do?

Did they use sex or bodies to sell their message?

# 17.
# PORNOGRAPHY

- WHAT IS PORNOGRAPHY?

- WHEN IS THE LAST TIME YOU SAW SOMETHING THAT WAS PORNOGRAPHIC?

- WHY IS PORNOGRAPHY DAMAGING TO INDIVIDUALS AND RELATIONSHIPS?

- WHY IS PORNOGRAPHY DAMAGING TO SOCIETY?

**PORNOGRAPHY:** *The portrayal of explicit sexual content for the purpose or intent of causing sexual arousal. In it, sex and bodies are commodified for the purpose of making a financial profit. Its most lucrative means of distribution is through the internet.*

## START THE CONVERSATION

Online porn is vastly different than anything parents grew up with. Children are exposed to pornography younger and younger, and people are forming attitudes about sex through porn. It's a huge influence as it trickles into and hypersexualizes all aspects of popular culture, including the media, toys, games, language, and attitudes.

IMost of our teenagers have been exposed to porn so it's important for us to approach it calmly and rationally. Don't freak out! Rather, ask them questions about their experience (see questions on next page). Explain that mixed reactions and feelings—being simultaneously repulsed, excited, disgusted, and aroused—are normal because of intense chemical reactions in the brain and body when viewing porn. Have a discussion about how the flood of intense pleasure chemicals can lead to addiction. If you feel it's appropriate, share with your kids any experience you've had with pornography and how it made you feel.

The use of porn is linked with increased callousness toward sex, decreased satisfaction with the person's real-life sexual partner, acceptance of the rape myth (that women like to and want to be raped), and disconnect from real-life relationships.

Explain how porn damages individuals. Just like with drugs and alcohol, teenage brains are ill-equipped to deal with porn. Extended pornography use affects the brain chemistry and can lead to addiction (see glossary), decreased empathy, dissatisfaction, and a diminished view of women. For more information, read one of our many online articles like 8 Harmful Effects of Pornography on Individuals.

Discuss how porn damages relationships. It can cause problems with trust. It desensitizes you to your partner's humanity and individuality. It puts the focus on your own pleasure and satisfaction without regard to your partner's. It's also important to note that the growing rate of erectile dysfunction in the male population is linked to prolonged exposure to and use of pornography (Voon, et. al., 2014). You may want to talk about this with your kids both now and when you discuss the Physical Response to Sex (topic #6).

Talk about how porn damages society. Millions of people viewing porn promotes the spread of rape culture (see glossary) and a focus on women in positions of powerlessness. It leads to a collective loss of empathy and the idea that women should always be sexually available. Because of the targeted efforts of the porn industry, pornography is more accessible and acceptable than ever. This has led to a hypersexualized culture where even food, pets, and children are sexualized.

More in-depth information on the effects of pornography can be found at www.educateempowerkids.org. Use our lessons and many articles to talk to kids of all ages about the dangers of online porn.

Also see our book *How to Talk to Your Kids About Pornography*, available on Amazon.

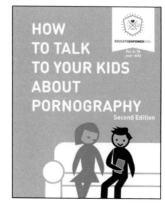

# ADDITIONAL QUESTIONS TO CONSIDER

When was the last time you saw pornography?

When was the first time you saw pornography?

How did seeing pornography make you feel?

How do your friends feel about porn?

Where are we most likely to encounter porn? At home? At school?

Have you ever been a situation that you were shown something pornographic and you felt uncomfortable, how did you handle it?

How could porn use affect your view of other people?

What are the crucial elements of healthy sex that porn destroys?

Some people seek out porn when bored, lonely, tired, sad, or stressed out. What do you do when you have these types of feelings? How do you cope?

# 18. MASTURBATION

- WHAT CONSTITUTES MASTURBATION?
- DO YOU FEEL THAT MASTURBATION IS HEALTHY? WHY OR WHY NOT?
- ARE THERE CONSEQUENCES TO MAKING IT A HABIT?

# START THE CONVERSATION

Talk about what masturbation is. Discuss your family values or opinions on masturbation and how your religion (if applicable) views masturbation without using shame or guilt. Discuss the role puberty may play in becoming interested in masturbation, such as boys having spontaneous erections and both boys and girls being flooded with new hormones.

Most kids masturbate because it feels good. However, sometimes they engage in compulsive masturbation because they have been sexually abused by an adult or peer. In this case, deeper resources and therapy may be necessary.

# ADDITIONAL QUESTIONS TO CONSIDER

Is it healthy to explore our bodies? Is there a difference between masturbating and exploring?

How can exploring our bodies make us feel more comfortable with ourselves?

What have you heard about using masturbation as a coping mechanism or an escape?

Why does it seem that our culture is more lenient towards boys masturbating than girls?

Do you think it can be a healthy habit or is it always wrong?

Should it replace a relationship?

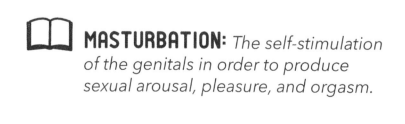

**MASTURBATION:** *The self-stimulation of the genitals in order to produce sexual arousal, pleasure, and orgasm.*

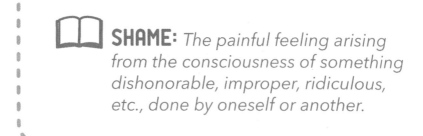

**SHAME:** *The painful feeling arising from the consciousness of something dishonorable, improper, ridiculous, etc., done by oneself or another.*

# START THE CONVERSATION

Many people associate sex with shame and guilt, and there are many reasons for it. But as we've said, sex is natural and awesome. Your children should know that, and you can help them understand that and remove any sense of shame and guilt they have about sex.

We have many common expressions using the word "dirt" for something bad: What's the "dirt" on that person, having a "dirty little secret." Discuss how that came to be with your kids (see the questions section below). Your teenager is going to be exposed to negative, counterfeit images of sex, but sex in and of itself, at the right time and with the right person, is a good and wonderful thing. Emphasize that we are sexual beings, and that's a good thing, but we have control over our actions.

Conflict between good physical feelings and going against social, religious, or parental teachings can cause shame and guilt.

Sexual assault can cause enormous feelings of shame, even though the victim is never at fault! There are lots of different forms of sexual assault, from unwanted touch to rape. See Unwanted Sexual Attention (topic #23). It's very important to emphasize that sexual assault is about power and violence, not sex, and certainly not healthy sexuality.

# 19.
# SHAME AND GUILT

- WHY DO SOME PEOPLE THINK SEX IS "BAD" OR "DIRTY?"

- WHY ARE WE CURIOUS ABOUT SEX?

- WHAT SITUATIONS COULD CAUSE GUILT OR SHAME ABOUT SEX?

- WHY IS IT COMMON FOR SEXUAL ASSAULT VICTIMS TO FEEL SHAME WHEN THE ABUSE IS NEVER THEIR FAULT?

Talk about what steps could be taken to avoid and resolve feelings of shame. Help your teenager understand that shame is associated with deeply negative feelings toward oneself. Shame focuses on "I am bad," while guilt focuses on "I did something bad or made a mistake." Guilt can be healthy and is easier to resolve. See the questions section below for ideas.

# ADDITIONAL QUESTIONS TO CONSIDER

How did sex become "dirty"?

What are society's standards for sex?

Does our family agree with society's standards?

Do society's standards correspond to your beliefs?

How is sex portrayed on TV: is it normal and healthy?

Does the portrayal of sex on TV reflect our family's feelings about sex?

Why is it natural to be curious about sex?

Is it okay for girls and boys to become aroused?

What can help us understand that sex is a wonderful, positive thing?

Is it okay to use and abuse sex for various reasons?

Under what circumstances can you feel good about having sex?

What are your requirements for a sexual relationship?

What will you do if you feel ashamed or guilty about something you've done or seen?

Who could you talk to if you have feelings of shame?

How do we overcome feelings of guilt or shame?

How can we gain a positive attitude about sex if we have previously had fearful or shameful feelings toward it?

Sometimes a victim of sexual abuse may feel shame and other negative feelings about themselves in relation to sex. How can they reclaim a sense of healthy sexuality?

# 20.
# SEXTING AND SOCIAL MEDIA

- ♛ WHAT IS SEXTING?

- ♛ WHAT SHOULD YOU DO IF YOU RECEIVE SEXT MESSAGES OR IMAGES?

- ♛ WHY DO PEOPLE FEEL THEY CAN SAY THINGS ON SOCIAL MEDIA THAT THEY WOULD NEVER SAY FACE TO FACE?

**SEXTING:** *The sending or distribution of sexually explicit images, messages, or other material via mobile phones.*

## START THE CONVERSATION

Sexting has become very prevalent in American culture among adults AND teens.

The legal ramifications of sexting are such that even an innocent receiver of a nude picture can get in trouble for having it. It is considered child pornography if it depicts naked pictures of people under 18 years old, and child pornography is illegal. Legal consequences for having or distributing it could fall under child pornography or child exploitation laws. A person who has been found with it may face jail time and/or being on the sex offender registry.

The explosion of social media has also given rise to an explosion of a free-for-all mentality. People frequently share opinions, thoughts, and comments unchecked. People can be blunt, rude, and callous in their use of social media. Explain how using primarily social media, texting, and other electronic communication to "interact" with others causes a disconnect between people, a sense of distance and removal, that can lead to this type of behavior online.

Social media has been linked to increased anxiety, feelings of inadequacy, depression, and feelings associated with poor body image. This is in large part because kids use social media to compare their worst to others' curated, filtered images.

"Show," don't "tell" your kids how to be good digital citizens by being kind and respectful in your own social media interactions.

• Show your kids how to handle a disagreement on social media.

• Show your kids healthy and unhealthy examples of social media use.

• Teach them to be thoughtful.

• Encourage as much face-to-face interaction as possible with your kids and their friends--including group dating--as a balance to their online socialization.

Remind your kids, EVERYTHING shared on social media can make an impact that you would never expect.

# ADDITIONAL QUESTIONS TO CONSIDER

What do your friends think of sexting? Have you or any of your friends been asked to send nudes? Have any of your friends asked for nude photos from a classmate?

How do you think a person feels when someone requests or demands a partially or fully nude photo of them?

How do you think people feel if they have received a sext message?

How do you think people feel when it has been shared?

Once you have sent a photo, can you ever get it back? Do you really think a teen who has asked for a nude photo will keep it to himself?

What will you do and who will you tell if you receive a sext message?

There seems to be a double standard in our culture where people do not shame a boy for requesting a nude photo of a girl, but a girl is shamed for sending one. Why does this double standard exist?

What makes people think they can say anything they want on social media, regardless of the effects?

What is appropriate use and behavior on social media? What behavior is not okay?

What are some ways we can help and uplift others with social media?

Are you the same person online/on social media that you are in real life?

How can you nurture real-life relationships?

What kind of face-to-face time is needed to establish and maintain a healthy relationship?

How will you balance your electronic communications with "the real thing?"

# SURVEY 2 **12+**

Please reflect on your discussions with your child up to this point and answer the following questions.

1. Select the topic that has been the most difficult to discuss with your child.

   11. Creating a Healthy Relationship
   12. Abusive Relationships
   13. Self-Esteem and Sex
   14. Liking Yourself
   15. Body Image and Sex
   16. Being Media Savvy
   17. Pornography
   18. Masturbation
   19. Shame and Guilt
   20. Sexting and Social Media


2. Referring to question 1, why was this topic difficult to discuss?
   _____
   _____


3. What have you said that has surprised you or exceeded your expectations of yourself in some way during the recent discussions?
   _____
   _____


4. What have you learned about your child during the recent discussions?
   _____
   _____

If you scan the code below, you can take this survey online. This will help us improve our curriculum and create new resources for parents.

# 21.
# SEXUAL
# CONVERSATIONS

- ♛ DO YOU THINK IT IS APPROPRIATE FOR AN ADULT OTHER THAN YOUR PARENTS TO DISCUSS SEX WITH YOU?

- ♛ WHEN IT COMES TO SEX, WHAT ARE KIDS TALKING ABOUT?

- ♛ ARE THESE CONVERSATIONS HELPFUL?

 **APPROPRIATE:** *Suitable, proper, or fitting for a particular purpose, person, or circumstance.*

## START THE CONVERSATION

Validate your kids' feelings if they're uncomfortable talking about sex with you, but remind them that you're empowering them with knowledge and that sex is a good and healthy thing. Talking about sex with your teenagers is essential because you want them to have accurate information and to understand the relational and emotional components of sex, which they are not likely to find in pop culture.

Let your teenagers know that sex is a natural and important part of life that deserves time and discussion. Tell them: We as your parents will answer your questions and concerns with accurate information. If there is something we don't know, we will find out together. Discuss which people, beside yourself, you feel are appropriate to talk to them about sex (a doctor at an appointment, a health teacher in a health class, etc.). Teach your kids where they can find useful information about sex (anatomy books, etc.). Remind them that innocent searches for information about sex will usually take them to porn sites.

## ADDITIONAL QUESTIONS TO CONSIDER

Why is getting information about sex from other teenagers not always a good choice?

When it comes to talking about sex with your parents, are these conversations awkward, interesting, helpful, or something else?

Is it only appropriate for you to talk with me, your parent, about sex?

Do you have any trusted adults you could talk to about sex?

Is it okay to talk to people online about sex?

# 22.
# SEXUAL IDENTIFICATION

- **IT IS INDIVIDUAL**

- **UNDERSTAND THAT SEXUALITY CAN BE FLUID, CHANGING OVER TIME; IT CAN ALSO BE CONSTANT**

- **YOUR SEXUALITY IS AN INTEGRAL PART OF YOU BUT IT DOES NOT DEFINE WHO YOU ARE**

- **WHAT ARE SOME FACTORS THAT CAN INFLUENCE YOUR SEXUALITY?**

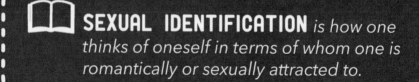

**SEXUAL IDENTIFICATION** *is how one thinks of oneself in terms of whom one is romantically or sexually attracted to.*

# START THE CONVERSATION

Our culture has become more open and accepting of different sexualities. Your kids are hearing a lot more about it than you likely did. As it's become part of the mainstream, it's important to discuss different aspects of sexual identification with your kids. Direct the conversation according to your beliefs and opinions and what you want your kids to know.

See the glossary for definitions of straight/heterosexual, gay, lesbian, bisexual, and transgender sexual identifications and discuss them.

Teach your teens that their sexuality is not the sum total of who they are. Although it influences all parts of their lives, sexuality is just one part of those lives.

Sexuality continues to develop during the teenage years. Tell your teen: Your experiences should not be based on what you've seen in pornography or in sexualized media. You have a right to create your own sexuality, have your own special experiences when the time is right, and formulate your own natural responses. A great resource for talking about this further is available in our online article, Why We Need to Fight for Our Kids' Healthy Sexuality.

# ADDITIONAL QUESTIONS TO CONSIDER

What does LGBTQI stand for?

What are your thoughts about different sexual identities?

Are there kids in your school who are trans, gay, bi etc.? How are they treated?

How can sexuality be fluid? What does that mean?

What are the benefits of creating your own sexual identity?

# 23.
# UNWANTED SEXUAL ATTENTION

- ♛ **WHAT CONSTITUTES UNWANTED SEXUAL ATTENTION?**

- 💬 **TELLING THE PERSON TO STOP IS YOUR RIGHT**

- 💬 **SOME SEXUAL ATTENTION OR BEHAVIORS ARE ILLEGAL**

# START THE CONVERSATION

Define unwanted sexual attention. It is a person giving you any sexually-based attention that you do not want. This could be verbal or physical. Explain that it can come from can come form anyone (acquaintances or strangers) or *anywhere*, including church, school, work, etc. Regardless of the source, giving attention that is not wanted is not okay.

Talk about strategies for your teens to be aware of their surroundings and who is around them when they're in public places. Emphasize that there is no circumstance in which it is okay for someone to give them sexual attention that they don't want. Remind your kids that most unwanted sexual attention and abuse come from people we know not from strangers.

There are many sexual behaviors that are illegal. They include exposing your genitals in public, an adult having sex with a minor, and rape. Refer back to the information covered in Consent (topic #10) for more information on rape and rape culture.

An informative resource on rape culture is at:
http://www.marshall.edu/wcenter/sexual-assault/rape-culture/
Additional discussion in Consent (topic #10).

**SEXUAL HARASSMENT:** *Harassment involving unwanted sexual advances or obscene remarks. Sexual harassment can be a form of sexual coercion as well as an undesired sexual proposition, including the promise of reward in exchange for sexual favors.*

An excellent resource to teach your kids about consent can be found in our online lesson "Talking to Your Kids About Consent."

## ADDITIONAL QUESTIONS TO CONSIDER

What is the difference between a flirtatious compliment and unwanted sexual attention?

Why might a person give another attention that's clearly not wanted?

What are some examples of unwanted sexual attention? (saying sexual things, whistling at someone, asking for nude photos, touching someone's body without permission, etc.)

How does pornography and our hypersexualized culture factor into people's ideas about sexual attention?

How can you keep yourself safe?

What would you say and do if a stranger, friend, or someone you are dating is giving you unwanted sexual attention?

Is it okay to tell the person to stop, even if it's a teacher, a coach, a member of the clergy, or a relative?

Is it okay to defend yourself physically or verbally in order to get the person to stop?

If someone gives you unwanted sexual attention (physical or verbal) is this your fault?

# 24.
# HOW PREDATORS GROOM KIDS

- ♛ WHAT DOES IT MEAN FOR A PREDATOR TO GROOM?

- 💬 PREDATORS ARE OFTEN PEOPLE THE TEENAGER KNOWS

- 💬 PREDATORS MAY USE "INNOCENT," "AFFECTIONATE" TOUCH TO DESENSITIZE AND BUILD TRUST

- 💬 PREDATORS CAN BE YOUR PEERS OR OTHER TEENAGERS

**PREDATOR:** *A predator is technically an organism or being that hunts and then feeds on their prey. A sexual predator is someone who seeks to obtain sexual contact through "hunting." The term is often used to describe the deceptive and coercive methods used by people who commit sex crimes where there is a victim, such as rape or child abuse.*

## START THE CONVERSATION

Predators can't be identified by how they look. It can be an uncle, friend, someone else your kids know, a stranger–anyone. Most people are good, but there are predators in every culture and population. They can be found online, at school, at church, and within our families. Be aware and make your kids aware of the warning signs and dangers of predators and how they groom their victims.

Talk about what it means to groom (see glossary) a person for sexual abuse or molestation. It is essentially a predator incorporating himself into the teen's life through special attention, "test touching," and gradually eroding normal social boundaries in order to sexually abuse or molest the teen. More in-depth information about this can be found in our online article, 8 Ways a Predator Might Groom a Child.

**Make it clear that you will always listen to your teenagers and not brush off their concerns if they ever feel not quite right about an adult in their lives, no matter who it is. If your child reveals molestation or rape, take it seriously. Report it immediately.**

A predator may use several methods to groom a child or teen including:

- May use their position of authority to manipulate kids

- Manipulate a young person's need for love, attention, and affection

- Pay special attention to a child and make him feel special

- Touch your child in your presence to get you comfortable with their "affection" for your child

- Work to become a close friend of the family

- Might take advantage of a child's natural curiosity and sex by telling "dirty" jokes, showing him porn, or by playing sexual games

- Might present him or herself as a sympathetic listener when parents, friends, and other disappoint a child

Discuss instincts with your teenagers. We have instincts that guide us and tell us when something doesn't feel right. Encourage your children to understand and identify their instincts and trust them. Even though they aren't perfect, following your instincts can help keep you safe.

## ADDITIONAL QUESTIONS TO CONSIDER

What does a predator look like?

Why can it be difficult to stand up to adults?

Would it be less difficult or more difficult to stand up to a peer or older teen?

What is a "test touch"?

What would you do if you had an icky feeling about someone for no identifiable reason?

Is it okay to speak up if you don't feel quite right about someone?

What if that someone were a family friend?

Predators will usually single out a child/teen and try to spend time alone with him/her. What can you do to avoid being alone with a coach, member of clergy, teacher, or anyone that makes you feel uncomfortable?

What could you do if you fear someone you know is being groomed? Who could you tell?

## SAMPLE SCENARIO

Pose the following scenario to your teen to enhance the discussion and bring the subject into a real-life context: You're on the team and excited to be coached by Mr. M, a highly-regarded coach. Several older friends have been coached by him and their game improved tremendously. You're hoping for the same improvement. You're flattered when Coach M starts paying special attention to you and your techniques.

He says you're a natural and wants to help you improve your skills. He's always touching you, helping you get in correct form and guiding you physically through the motions he's trying to teach you. You're starting to feel a little uncomfortable about all the touching–it's kind of weird. Soon Coach M suggests setting up time after practice for the two of you to work together one on one. You feel very uncomfortable, even alarmed, at that idea. But he's this awesome coach. What will you do? Will you talk with someone you trust about your feelings? Will you suggest that a couple teammates join you? Will you ignore your misgivings and do it?

# 25.
# MONOGAMY VS. MULTIPLE PARTNERS

- ★ WHAT IS MONOGAMY?

- ★ WHAT ARE SOME EMOTIONAL AND SPIRITUAL BENEFITS OF MONOGAMY?

- ★ WHAT ARE SOME HEALTH BENEFITS OF MONOGAMY?

- ★ ARE THERE RISKS TO HAVING MULTIPLE PARTNERS?

**MONOGAMY:** *A relationship in which a person has one partner at any one time.*

# START THE CONVERSATION

Talk about your family values and tell your kids how you feel about monogamy and about having multiple partners. Decide before this conversation how you want to handle your kids' possible questions about your own sexual history. Also be prepared to handle and discuss anything your kids may want to reveal to you about their own experiences.

Talk about various benefits of monogamy according to your beliefs and values. A risk of having multiple partners is the possibility of contracting sexually transmitted diseases or infections. See the glossary for definitions of STDs and STIs.

We will discuss more about sexually transmitted diseases/infections in topic #29.

# ADDITIONAL QUESTIONS TO CONSIDER

What do you think of monogamy? How do your friends feel about monogamy?

Do all cultures believe in monogamy?

What are your thoughts about serial monogamy?

Do men and women feel differently about monogamy?

Does our culture have different beliefs regarding men who have multiple partners versus women who have multiple partners? Why is that?

Is it honest to have multiple partners at once without those partners knowing that's happening?

How does monogamy impact your emotions?

How does having multiple partners impact your emotions?

Are there benefits to having multiple partners?

Can STDs/STIs be avoided if you have multiple partners?

# 26.
# SEX IN A COMMITTED RELATIONSHIP VS. HOOK UP SEX

- ★ HOW DO YOU THINK SEX IN A COMMITTED RELATIONSHIP DIFFERS FROM HOOK UP SEX?

- ★ WHY DO PEOPLE IN COMMITTED RELATIONSHIPS HAVE SEX?

- ★ WHY DO PEOPLE HOOK UP TO HAVE SEX?

**HOOK UP SEX:** *A form of casual sex in which sexual activity takes place outside the context of a committed relationship. The sex may be a one-time event, or an ongoing arrangement; in either case, the focus is generally on the physical enjoyment of sexual activity without an emotional involvement or commitment.*

## START THE CONVERSATION

This discussion is meant to get your teens thinking more about what they want from a sexual relationship when the time is right. Guide it, as always, based on your opinions and values.

Sex in a committed relationship is very different from casual hook up sex. Discuss how shame and regret, a boosted ego, getting a reputation, stereotyping, etc., can be associated with hook up sex. Discuss the health risks involved in hook up sex, especially with multiple partners. Talk with your teens about health and emotional benefits of sex within a committed relationship. Discuss your family beliefs about sex within and outside of marriage.

Hook up sex is often promoted in pop culture as fun, easy, victimless, and without regrets. Discuss the realities of these pop culture ideas. Take a few minutes to share with your kids your thoughts and opinion about mobile apps such as Tinder and Grindr that promote hook ups between local strangers.

# ADDITIONAL QUESTIONS TO CONSIDER

How is sex in a committed relationship different from casual hook up sex?

What's present or absent in one that's not present or absent in the other?

Is there an emotional aspect to hook up sex?

Is there a social aspect to hook up sex?

Why do people have hook up sex?

How do you feel when you hear about someone you know having casual hook up sex?

Do you think everyone is doing it?

Why do people in a committed relationship have sex?

How do you feel about sex within a committed relationship among people your age?

Are there positives to hook up sex?

Have you heard of "revenge sex" (having sex with someone to get back at another person or make them jealous)? What are your thoughts on this?

# 27.
# THE DOUBLE STANDARD AND DEROGATORY SLANG TERMS

- WHAT ARE DEROGATORY TERMS THAT ARE USED FOR MEN? FOR WOMEN?

- HOW DO YOU FEEL WHEN YOU HEAR THEM?

- WHAT IS SLUT-SHAMING AND HOW DOES IT IMPACT WOMEN?

- WHAT IS THE SEXUAL DOUBLE STANDARD THAT EXISTS IN OUR CULTURE?

- DEROGATORY TERMS ARE MEANT TO HUMILIATE AND DEHUMANIZE

**DOUBLE STANDARD:** *A rule or standard that is applied differently and unfairly to a person or distinct groups of people.*

# START THE CONVERSATION

Start by talking about what a derogatory term is. Ask your teens for specific derogatory terms they've heard and what's meant by them, and decide if you think you should bring up any they haven't mentioned.

Tell your kids how you feel when you hear these words. Discuss ways they can cope with these terms when they hear them. Talk about misogyny (see glossary): what it is, where it may have come from, what your kids can do to stand up to it.

Slut-shaming is focusing on a girl's promiscuous sexual behavior, whether she is actually promiscuous or not (see glossary). A slut-shaming study with good information is at http://america. aljazeera.com/articles/2014/5/29/slut-shaming-study.html.

The classic sexual double standard is that men don't get bad sexual reputations, but women do for the same behavior and actions. Men and boys are typically praised for sexual contacts while women are controlled sexually through judgment, shame, and humiliation. Discuss reasons why there may be double standards. Discuss the double standard that existed in your teenage years.

The purpose of derogatory terms is to humiliate and dehumanize people. Open a discussion about the various reasons why people would want to do that and treat each other that way.

# ADDITIONAL QUESTIONS TO CONSIDER

Have you ever been called a derogatory name or term?

Have you ever used derogatory names or terms?

What were the circumstances under which you were called or used these words?

How did you handle it?

How did you feel about hearing or using derogatory words?

How does slut-shaming impact a girl's humanity and dignity?

Why would people use slut-shaming on girls who are not promiscuous or even sexually active?

Why are so many derogatory terms focused on women?

Why do some people want to humiliate and dehumanize others by using derogatory terms?

What can you say to someone who is talking about another person in that way?

In what way do you see double standards play out on an everyday basis?

Have you been treated or treated someone with a double standard?

What are strengths that men have?

What are strengths that women have?

Why do we need both men's and women's strengths?

Why do double standards exist?

What can you do to change or stand up to double standards?

LADIES MAN

SLUT

# 28.
# SEX UNDER THE INFLUENCE

- ♛ HOW DO ALCOHOL OR DRUGS AFFECT YOUR BEHAVIOR?

- 💬 ALCOHOL AND DRUGS IMPAIR YOUR ABILITY TO GIVE CONSENT OR RECEIVE CONSENT

- ♛ WHAT WOULD SEX UNDER THE INFLUENCE BE LIKE COMPARED TO SOBER SEX?

## START THE CONVERSATION

This is a very relevant topic for teenagers because it's so widespread. Adolescence is frequently a time when kids begin experimenting with drugs and alcohol and are given the opportunity to use them. Talking about it now will help your teens think more critically about it and make decisions for themselves before they're in a situation that could get out of hand.

Explain that people do things when drunk, high, or under the influence of a substance that they wouldn't otherwise do because alcohol and drugs impair judgment, physical coordination, and natural inhibitions and open the door to risky behaviors. Discuss your understanding of when someone should stop drinking (after one glass of wine, after two beers, etc.). Help your teen have a plan for avoiding drinking now and responsible drinking later.

Discuss how alcohol and drugs influence decision-making. Talk about consent, referring back to the discussion in Consent (topic #10) as needed.

Open a discussion about the emotional fallout of having sex with someone while under the influence of a drug or alcohol whom you'd never consider being with when sober. If applicable and if you feel it's appropriate, share any experiences that you have had with mixing alcohol and/or drugs with sex. Finally, teach

**UNDER THE INFLUENCE:** *Being physically affected by alcohol or drugs.*

your kids to have a safety plan when drinking, drugs, or other dangerous situations are present in their social engagements. Consider having a code word that your kids can text you. It may not even have to come from their phone number, and you will pick them up, no questions asked.

## ADDITIONAL QUESTIONS TO CONSIDER

How does someone who is drunk, high, or under the influence of drugs behave?

Have you seen someone do things when drunk or high that are out of character?

Can a person give consent or receive consent while they're drinking or doing drugs?

Can you connect emotionally with someone who is drunk, high, or otherwise under the influence?

Is there a difference between having sex when drunk or high versus having sex when sober?

What are some common drugs being used at your school?

## SAMPLE SCENARIO

Pose the following scenario to your teen to enhance the discussion and bring the subject into a real-life context: You're at a party and see a girl who is clearly drunk and not in control of herself. Two guys are gradually cornering her, getting closer and beginning to touch her casually. As you watch, they become more aggressive, grabbing her breasts and bottom. She doesn't seem to totally comprehend what's going on, but she does try weakly to move away from the guys. They continue in their actions anyway. Are you going to have the courage to speak up? What will you say?

# 29.
# STDs AND STIs

- ⚅ **DO YOU KNOW THE NAMES AND SYMPTOMS OF STDs AND STIs?**

- 💬 **SOME STDs AND STIs LAST A LIFETIME**

- 💬 **PREVENTION INCLUDES REGULAR CONDOM USE AND ABSTINENCE FOLLOWED BY MONOGAMY**

# START THE CONVERSATION

The CDC (Centers for Disease Control) estimates that there are 20 million annual new infections, 110 million total infections, and $16 billion in associated medical costs of sexually transmitted diseases and infections. This didn't just happen when people became adults. Speak with a doctor or health professional if your teens need help.

Discuss specific STDs and STIs, such as gonorrhea, chlamydia, herpes, syphilis, HPV, and HIV (see glossary). Talk about prevention. Share your ideas and values about prevention.

For in-depth information, we recommend you consult this resource:

http://www.womenshealth.gov/publications/our-publications/fact-sheet/sexually-transmitted-infections.html

# ADDITIONAL QUESTIONS TO CONSIDER

Do you know how various STDs and STIs affect the body?

Which can be cured with treatment?

Which cannot be cured with treatment?

**STD AND STI:** *An abbreviation that refers to sexually transmitted diseases or infections. These are illnesses that are communicable through sexual behaviors, including intercourse. Some of these illnesses can also be transmitted through blood contact.*

# 30.
# BIRTH
# CONTROL

- WHAT ARE THE VARIOUS METHODS OF BIRTH CONTROL?

- HAVING A BABY WHEN YOU'RE EMOTIONALLY AND FINANCIALLY READY IS POSITIVE AND EXTRAORDINARY

- THE ONLY 100% EFFECTIVE BIRTH CONTROL METHOD IS ABSTINENCE

**CONTRACEPTIVE:** *A method, device, or medication that works to prevent pregnancy. Another name for birth control.*

## START THE CONVERSATION

Your family values and religious (if applicable) standards are very important regarding birth control. Guide this conversation, as all the others, according to what you feel is important for your teenagers to know and understand.

Talk about different forms of birth control, such as the pill, patch, implant, shot, IUD, diaphragm, condoms, and the rhythm method (see glossary).

In 2013, the teenage pregnancy rate was 26.6 births for every 1,000 female teenagers between the ages of 15 and 19. Of these, almost 89% occurred outside of marriage.

Have a discussion about having a family under the best circumstances and what you and your teens think the best circumstances are.

If your teen needs help or medical care, speak with a doctor or health professional. For in-depth information, we recommend you consult this resource:

http://www.mayoclinic.org/healthy-living/birth-control/basics/birth-control-basics/hlv-20049454

# ADDITIONAL QUESTIONS TO CONSIDER

Why do people consider birth control an inconvenience considering how easy it is?

Why do people avoid wearing condoms?

What will you do if your partner tries to pressure you to have sex without him wearing a condom OR without her using some form of birth control?

Why are there still debates about birth control when it's so easy to get, and many times free?

What are some ineffective methods of birth control? (pulling out before ejaculation, the rhythm method, etc.)

What do you think of teen birth rate statistics in light of so many available birth control methods?

Are there positive aspects to being an unmarried teenage parent?

What are the best circumstances under which to have a family?

What is the best family situation for the baby?

What is the best family situation for the parents?

What are the benefits to each family member in waiting to have a baby until these circumstances are in place?

# SURVEY 3 **12+**

Thank you for using 30 Days of Sex Talks. Please answer the following questions to help us continue to improve our program.

1. Did you use the sample dialogues and/or activities during your discussions?

   Yes                    No

2. Referring to question 1, which dialogues and/or activities worked best and worst for your child?

   Best_____

   Worst_____

3. Please select the topic (if any) that was the most difficult to discuss.

   1. The Physical Side of Relationships
   2. Sex
   3. Emotional Intimacy
   4. Sex Means Different Things to Boys and Girls
   5. Positive Aspects of Sex
   6. Physical Responses to Sex
   7. Orgasm
   8. Relationship Boundaries
   9. The First Time
   10. Consent
   11. Creating a Healthy Relationship
   12. Abusive Relationships
   13. Self-Esteem and Sex
   14. Liking Yourself
   15. Body Image and Sex
   16. Being Media Savvy
   17. Pornography
   18. Masturbation
   19. Shame and Guilt
   20. Sexting and Social Media

21. Sexual Conversations
22. Sexual Identification
23. Unwanted Sexual Attention
24. How Predators Groom Kids
25. Monogamy vs. Multiple Partners
26. Sex in a Committed Relationship vs. Hook-up Sex
27. The Double Standard and Derogatory Slang Terms
28. Sex Under the Influence
29. STDs/STIs
30. Birth Control

4. Referring to question 3, why was this topic difficult to discuss?

_____

_____


5. Having completed this program, please rate your current comfort level of discussing human sexuality with your child.

1    2    3    4    5    6    7    8    9    10

Low                    Medium                    High


6. Do you feel that your ability to discuss difficult things with your child has been enhanced by these discussions? Please explain your answer.

Yes                    No

_____

_____


7. Was there anything that you learned from your child that surprised you (good or bad)? Please describe below.

_____

_____

8. Do you feel that this experience has increased the likelihood of your child coming to you with questions about sex and sexuality?

Yes                    No


9. Rate the effectiveness of the overall program below.

1    2    3    4    5    6    7    8    9    10

Low                        Medium                        High


10. Would you recommend this program to your friends and family?

Yes                    No


11. Is there anything that you think the program needs to improve, add, or remove? If so, please explain.


**If you scan the code below, you can take this survey online. This will help us improve our curriculum and create new resources for parents.**

# FREE DOWNLOADABLE!

This curriculum works best when it is interactive between you and your child. To help facilitate this interaction, we've developed topic cards as a companion to this book. The topic cards are a bonus for you to download at your convenience. They can be printed and placed on the refrigerator, on a mirror, in your pocket or wherever they need to be to serve as a reminder to both you and your child to **start talking!**

**To obtain your free download, please scan the QR code below and enter the following password: 7ygvBHU\***

# IF YOU ENJOYED THIS BOOK, PLEASE LEAVE A POSITIVE REVIEW ON AMAZON.COM

For great resources and information, follow us on our social media outlets:

Facebook: www.facebook.com/educateempowerkids/
Twitter: @EduEmpowerKids
Pinterest: pinterest.com/educateempower/
Instagram: Eduempowerkids

Subscribe to our website for exclusive offers and information at: www.educateempowerkids.org

# REFERENCES AND RESOURCES

## Strengthening your child
30 Days to a Stronger Child, http://amzn.to/25t8l0J

## Talking to kids about pornography
How to Talk to Your Kids About Pornography, http://amzn.to/1OjQKfA

Hilton, D., & Watts, C. (2011, February 21). Pornography addiction: A neuroscience perspective. Retrieved from http://www.ncbi.nlm.nih.gov/pmc/articles/PMC3050060/

Layden, M. (n.d.). Pornography and Violence: A New Look at Research. Retrieved from http://www.socialcostsofpornography.com/Layden_Pornography_and_Violence.pdf

Voon, V. et. al. (2014, July 11). Neural Correlates of Sexual Cue Reactivity in Individuals with and without Compulsive Sexual Behaviours. Retrieved from http://www.plosone.org/article/info%3Adoi%2F10.1371%2Fjournal.pone.0102419

## Rape culture resource
http://www.marshall.edu/wcenter/sexual-assault/rape-culture/

## Predator-victim grooming resource
http://www.parenting.org/article/victim-grooming-protect-your-child-from-sexual-predators

## Slut-shaming study
http://america.aljazeera.com/articles/2014/5/29/slut-shaming-study.html

## Birth control resource
http://www.mayoclinic.org/healthy-living/birth-control/basics/birth-control-basics/hlv-20049454

## Pregnancy rates
http://www.hhs.gov/ash/oah/adolescent-health-topics/reproductive-health/teen-pregnancy/trends.html#.VBy66hB0ypo

**Pregnancy resource**
https://www.whattoexpect.com

**STD/STI resource**
http://www.womenshealth.gov/publications/our-publications/
fact-sheet/sexually-transmitted-infections.html

**STD/STI rates**
http://www.cdc.gov/std/stats/STI-Estimates-Fact-Sheet-
Feb-2013.pdf

**Domestic violence resource**
http://www.justice.gov/ovw/domestic-violence

**Domestic violence resource**
http://www.thehotline.org/

**Information on masturbation and porn use**
http://blogs.psychcentral.com/sex/2011/04/compulsive-mastur-
bation-and-porn/

**Creating a family media standard**
http://bit.ly/1xwb1ri

**Lesson on Media Literacy**
https://educateempowerkids.org/lesson-media-literacy

**Videos related to the 30 Days of Sex Talks books**
http://bit.ly/29zyVNW

# GLOSSARY

*The following terms have been included to assist you as you prepare and hold discussions with your children regarding healthy sexuality and intimacy. The definitions are not intended for the child; rather, they are meant to clarify the concepts and terms for the adult. Some terms may not be appropriate for your child, given their age, circumstances, or your own family culture and values. Use your judgment to determine which terminology best meets your individual needs.*

**Abstinence**: The practice of not doing or having something that is wanted or enjoyable: the practice of abstaining from something.

**Abuse:** The improper usage or treatment of another person or entity, often to unfairly gain power or other benefit in the relationship.

**Affection:** A feeling or type of love that exceeds general goodwill.

**AIDS:** A sexually transmitted or bloodborne viral infection that causes immune deficiency.

**Anal Sex:** A form of intercourse that generally involves the insertion and thrusting of the erect penis into the anus or rectum for sexual pleasure.

**Anus:** The external opening of the rectum comprised of two sphincters which control the exit of feces from the body.

**Appropriate:** Suitable, proper, or fitting for a particular purpose, person, or circumstance.

**Arousal:** The physical and emotional response to sexual desire during or in anticipation of sexual activity.

**Bisexual:** Sexual orientation in which one is attracted to both males and females.

**Body Image:** An individual's feelings regarding their own physical attractiveness and sexuality. These feelings and opinions are often influenced by other people and media sources.

**Bodily Integrity:** The personal belief that our bodies, while crucial to our understanding of who we are, do not in themselves solely define our worth; the knowledge that our bodies are the storehouse of our humanity; and the sense that we esteem our bodies and we treat them accordingly.

**Boundaries:** The personal limits or guidelines that an individual forms in order to clearly identify what are reasonable and safe behaviors for others to engage in around him or her.

**Bowel Movement:** Also known as defecation, a bowel movement is the final act of digestion by which waste is eliminated from the body via the anus.

**Breasts:** Women develop breasts on their upper torso during puberty. Breasts contain mammary glands, which create the breast milk used to feed infants.

**Child:** A person between birth and full growth.

**Chlamydia:** Bacteria that causes or is associated with various diseases of the eye and urogenital tract.

**Clitoris:** A female sex organ visible at the front juncture of the labia minora above the opening of the urethra. The clitoris is the female's most sensitive erogenous zone.

**Condom:** A thin rubber covering that a man wears on his penis during sex in order to prevent a woman from becoming pregnant or to prevent the spread of diseases.

**Consent:** Clear agreement or permission to permit something or to do something. Consent must be given freely, without force or intimidation, and while the person is fully conscious and cognizant of their present situation.

**Contraceptive:** A method, device, or medication that works to prevent pregnancy. Another name for birth control.

**Curiosity:** The desire to learn or know more about something or someone.

**Date Rape:** A rape in which the perpetrator has a relationship that is, to some degree, either romantic or potentially sexual with the victim. The perpetrator uses physical force, psychological intimidation, or drugs or alcohol to force the victim to have sex either against their will or in a state in which they cannot give clear consent.

**Degrade:** To treat with contempt or disrespect.

**Demean:** To cause a severe loss in the dignity of or respect for another person.

**Derogatory:** An adjective that implies severe criticism or loss of respect.

**Diaphragm:** A cervical barrier type of birth control made of a soft latex or silicone dome with a spring molded into the rim. The spring creates a seal against the walls of the vagina, preventing semen, including sperm, from entering the fallopian tubes.

**Domestic Abuse/Domestic Violence:** A pattern of abusive behavior in any relationship that is used by one partner to gain or maintain power and control over another intimate partner. It can be physical, sexual, emotional, economic, or psychological actions or threats of actions that influence another person. (DOJ definition)

**Double Standard:** A rule or standard that is applied differently and unfairly to a person or distinct groups of people.

**Egg Cell:** The female reproductive cell, which, when fertilized by sperm inside the uterus, will eventually grow into an infant.

**Ejaculation:** When a man reaches orgasm, during which semen is expelled from the penis.

**Emotional Abuse:** A form of abuse in which another person is subjected to behavior that can result in psychological trauma. Emotional abuse often occurs within relationships in which there is a power imbalance.

**Emotional Intimacy:** As aspect of relationships that is dependent upon trust and that can be expressed both verbally and non-verbally. Emotional intimacy displays a degree of closeness that exceeds that normally experienced in common relational interactions.

**Epididymal Hypertension:** A condition that results from prolonged sexual arousal in human males in which fluid congestion in the testicles occurs, often accompanied by testicular pain. The condition is temporary. Also referred to as "blue balls."

**Erection:** During a penile erection, the penis becomes engorged and enlarged due to the dilation of the cavernosal arteries (which run the length of the penis) and subsequent engorgement of the surrounding corporal tissue with blood.

**Explicit:** An adjective signifying that something is stated clearly, without room for confusion or doubt. Sexually explicit material, however, signifies that the content contains sexual material that may be considered offensive or overtly graphic.

**Extortion:** To obtain something through force or via threats.

**Family:** A group consisting of parents and children living together in a household. The definition of family is constantly evolving, and every person can define family in a different way to encompass the relationships he or she shares with people in his or her life. Over time one's family will change as one's life changes and the importance of family values and rituals deepen.

**Female Arousal:** The physiological responses to sexual desire during or in anticipation of sexual activity in women include vaginal lubrication (wetness), engorgement of the external genitals (clitoris and labia), enlargement of the vagina, and dilation of the pupils.

**Fertilize:** The successful union between an egg (technically known as the ovum) and a sperm, which normally occurs within the second portion of the fallopian tube (known as the ampulla). The result of fertilization is a zygote (fertilized egg).

**Friend:** Someone with whom a person has a relationship of mutual affection. A friend is closer than an associate or acquaintance. Friends typically share emotions and characteristics such as affection, empathy, honesty, trust, and compassion.

**Gay:** A word used to describe people who are sexually attracted to members of the same sex. The term "lesbian" is generally preferred when talking about women who are attracted to other women. Originally, the word "gay" meant "carefree"; its connection to sexual orientation developed during the latter half of the 20th century.

**Gender:** Masculinity and femininity are differentiated through a range of characteristics known as "gender." They may include biological sex (being male or female), social roles based upon biological sex, and one's subjective experience and understanding of their own gender identity.

**Gender Role:** The pattern of masculine or feminine behavior of an individual that is defined by a particular culture and that is largely determined by a child's upbringing.

**Gender Stereotypes:** A thought or understanding applied to either males or females (or other gender identities) that may or may not correspond with reality. "Men don't cry" or "women are weak" are examples of inaccurate gender stereotypes.

**Gestation:** The time when a person or animal is developing inside its mother before it is born.

**Gonorrhea:** A contagious inflammation of the genital mucous membrane caused by the gonococcus.

**Groom:** To prepare or train someone for a particular purpose or activity. In the case of sexual predators, it is any willful action made by the offender to prepare the victim and/or the victim's support network that allows for easier sex offending.

**Healthy Sexuality:** Having the ability to express one's sexuality in ways that contribute positively to one's own self-esteem and relationships. Healthy sexuality includes approaching sexual relationships and interactions with mutual agreement and dignity. It necessarily includes mutual respect and a lack of fear, shame, or guilt, and never includes coercion or violence.

**Hepatitis B:** A sometimes fatal disease caused by a double-stranded DNA virus that tends to persist in the blood serum and is transmitted especially by contact with infected blood (as by transfusion or by sharing contaminated needles in illicit intravenous drug use) or by contact with other infected bodily fluids such as semen.

**Hepatitis C:** Caused by a single-stranded RNA virus of the family Flaviviridae that tends to persist in the blood serum and is usually transmitted by infected blood (as by injection of an illicit drug, blood transfusion, or exposure to blood or blood products).

**Herpes:** Any of several inflammatory diseases of the skin caused by herpes viruses and characterized by clusters of vesicles.

**Heterosexual:** Sexual orientation in which one is attracted to members of the opposite sex (males are attracted to females; females are attracted to males).

**HIV:** Any of several retroviruses and especially HIV-1 that infect and destroy helper T cells of the immune system causing the marked reduction in their numbers that is diagnostic of AIDS.

**Homosexual:** Sexual orientation in which one is attracted to members of the same sex (males are attracted to males; females are attracted to females).

**Hook up Sex:** A form of casual sex in which sexual activity takes place outside the context of a committed relationship. The sex may be a one-time event, or an ongoing arrangement; in either case, the focus is generally on the physical enjoyment of sexual activity without an emotional involvement or commitment.

**HPV:** Human papillomavirus.

**Hymen:** A membrane that partially closes the opening of the vagina and whose presence is traditionally taken to be a mark of virginity. However, it can often be broken before a woman has sex simply by being active, and sometimes it is not present at all.

**Hyper-sexualized:** To make extremely sexual; to accentuate the sexuality of. Often seen in media.

**Instinct:** An inherent inclination towards a particular behavior. Behavior that is performed without being based on prior experience is instinctive.

**Intercourse:** Sexual activity, also known as coitus or copulation, which is most commonly understood to refer to the insertion of the penis into the vagina (vaginal sex). It should be noted that there are a wide range of various sexual activities and the boundaries of what constitutes sexual intercourse are still under debate.

**Intimacy:** Generally a feeling or form of significant closeness. There are four types of intimacy: physical intimacy (sensual proximity or touching), emotional intimacy (close connection resulting from trust and love), cognitive or intellectual intimacy (resulting from honest exchange of thoughts and ideas), and experiential intimacy (a connection that occurs while acting together). Emotional and physical intimacy are often associated with sexual relationships, while intellectual and experiential intimacy are not.

**Labia:** The inner and outer folds of the vulva on both sides of the vagina.

**Lesbian:** A word used to describe women who are sexually attracted to other women.

**Lice (Pubic):** A sucking louse infesting the pubic region of the human body.

**Love:** A wide range of emotional interpersonal connections, feelings, and attitudes. Common forms include kinship or familial love, friendship, divine love (as demonstrated through worship), and sexual or romantic love. In biological terms, love is the attraction and bonding that functions to unite human beings and facilitate the social and sexual continuation of the species.

**Masturbation:** The self-stimulation of the genitals in order to produce sexual arousal, pleasure, and orgasm.

**Media Literacy:** The ability to study, understand, and create messages in various media such as books, social media posts, and photos, movies, games, music, news stories, online ads, blog posts, school essays, etc.

**Menstrual Cycle:** Egg is released from ovaries through fallopian tube into uterus. Each month, blood and tissue build up in the uterus. When the egg is not fertilized, this blood and tissue are not needed and are shed from the body through the vagina. Cycle is roughly 28 days but can vary. Bleeding time lasts from 2-7 days. May be accompanied by cramping, breast tenderness, and emotional sensitivity.

**Menstrual Period:** A discharging of blood, secretions, and tissue debris from the uterus at periods of approximately one month in females of breeding age that are not pregnant.

**Misogyny:** The hatred, aversion, hostility, or dislike of women or girls. Misogyny can appear in a single individual, or may also be manifest in broad cultural trends that undermine women's autonomy and value.

**Monogamy:** A relationship in which a person has one partner at any one time.

**Nipples:** The circular, somewhat conical structure of tissue on the breast. The skin of the nipple and its surrounding areola are often several shades darker than that of the surrounding breast tissue. In women, the nipple delivers breast milk to infants.

**Nocturnal Emissions** A spontaneous orgasm that occurs during sleep. Nocturnal emissions can occur in both males (ejaculation) and females (lubrication of the vagina). The term "wet dream" is often used to describe male nocturnal emissions.

**Nudity:** The state of not wearing any clothing. Full nudity denotes a complete absence of clothing, while partial nudity is a more ambiguous term, denoting the presence of an indeterminate amount of clothing.

**Oral Sex:** Sexual activity that involves stimulation of the genitals through the use of another person's mouth.

**Orgasm:** The rhythmic muscular contractions in the pelvic region that occur as a result of sexual stimulation, arousal, and activity during the sexual response cycle. Orgasms are characterized by a sudden release of built-up sexual tension and by the resulting sexual pleasure.

**Penis:** The external male sexual organ comprised of the shaft, foreskin, glans penis, and meatus. The penis contains the urethra, through which both urine and semen travel to exit the body.

**Perception:** A way of regarding, understanding, or interpreting something; a mental impression

**Period:** The beginning of the menstrual cycle.

**Physical Abuse:** The improper physical treatment of another person or entity designed to cause bodily harm, pain, injury, or other suffering. Physical abuse is often employed to unfairly gain power or other benefit in the relationship.

**The Pill:** An oral contraceptive for women containing the hormones estrogen and progesterone or progesterone alone, that inhibits ovulation, fertilization, or implantation of a fertilized ovum, causing temporary infertility. Common brands include Ortho Tri-Cyclen, Yasmin, and Ortho-Novum.

**Pornography:** The portrayal of explicit sexual content for the purpose or intent of causing sexual arousal. In it, sex and bodies are commodified for the purpose of making a financial profit. It can be created in a variety of media contexts, including videos, photos, animation, books and magazines. Its most lucrative means of distribution is through the internet. The industry that creates pornography is a sophisticated, corporatized, billion dollar business.

**Positive Self-Talk:** Anything said to oneself for encouragement or motivation, such as phrases or mantras; also, one's ongoing internal conversation with oneself, like a running commentary, which influences how one feels and behaves.

**Predator:** A predator is technically an organism or being that hunts and then feeds on their prey. A sexual predator is someone who seeks to obtain sexual contact through "hunting." The term is often used to describe the deceptive and coercive methods used by people who commit sex crimes where there is a victim, such as rape or child abuse.

**Pregnancy:** The common term used for gestation in humans. During pregnancy, the embryo or fetus grows and develops inside a woman's uterus.

**Premature Ejaculation:** When a man regularly reaches orgasm, during which semen is expelled from the penis, prior to or within one minute of the initiation of sexual activity.

**Priapism:** The technical term of a condition in which the erect penis does not return to flaccidity within four hours, despite the absence of physical or psychological sexual stimulation.

**Private:** Belonging to or for the use of a specific individual. Private and privacy denote a state of being alone, solitary, individual, exclusive, secret, personal, hidden, and confidential.

**Psychological Abuse:** A form of abuse in which a person is subjected to behavior that can result in psychological trauma. Psychological abuse often occurs within relationships in which there is a power imbalance.

**Puberty:** A period or process through which children reach sexual maturity. Once a person has reached puberty, their body is capable of sexual reproduction.

**Public:** Belonging to or for the use of all people in a specific area, or all people as a whole. Something that is public is common, shared, collective, communal, and widespread.

**Rape:** A sex crime in which the perpetrator forces another person to have sexual intercourse against their will and without consent. Rape often occurs through the threat or actuality of violence against the victim.

**Rape Culture:** A culture in which rape is pervasive and to an extent normalized due to cultural and societal attitudes towards gender and sexuality. Behaviors that facilitate rape culture include victim blaming, sexual objectification, and denial regarding sexual violence.

**Relationship:** The state of being connected with another person or the way in which two people are connected.

**Rhythm Method:** A method of avoiding pregnancy by restricting sexual intercourse to the times of a woman's menstrual cycle when ovulation and conception are least likely to occur. Because it can be difficult to predict ovulation and because abstinence has to be practiced for up to ten days of a woman's cycle, the effectiveness of the rhythm method is on average just 75–87%, according to http://www.webmd.com.

**Romantic Love:** A form of love that denotes intimacy and a strong desire for emotional connection with another person to whom one is generally also sexually attracted.

**Scrotum:** The pouch of skin underneath the penis that contains the testicles.

**Self-Esteem / Self -Worth:** An individual's overall emotional evaluation of their own worth. Self-esteem is both a judgment of the self and an attitude toward the self. More generally, the term is used to describe a confidence in one's own value or abilities.

**Semen:** The male reproductive fluid, which contains spermatozoa in suspension. Semen exits the penis through ejaculation.

**Serial Monogamy:** A mating system in which a man or woman can only form a long-term, committed relationship (such as marriage) with one partner at a time. Should the relationship dissolve, the individual may go on to form another relationship, but only after the first relationship has ceased.

**Sexting:** The sending or distribution of sexually explicit images, messages, or other material via mobile phones.

**Sexual Abuse:** The improper sexual usage or treatment of another person or entity, often to unfairly gain power or other benefit in the relationship. In instances of sexual abuse, undesired sexual behaviors are forced upon one person by another.

**Sexual Assault:** A term often used in legal contexts to refer to sexual violence. Sexual assault occurs when there is any non-consensual sexual contact or violence. Examples include rape, groping, forced kissing, child sexual abuse, and sexual torture.

**Sexual Harassment:** Harassment involving unwanted sexual advances or obscene remarks. Sexual harassment can be a form of sexual coercion as well as an undesired sexual proposition, including the promise of reward in exchange for sexual favors.

**Sexual Identification:** How one thinks of oneself in terms of whom one is romantically or sexually attracted to.

**Sexual Molestation:** Aggressive and persistent harassment, either psychological or physical, of a sexual manner.

**Shame:** The painful feeling arising from the consciousness of something dishonorable, improper, ridiculous, etc., done by oneself or another.

**Slut-shaming:** The act of criticizing, attacking, or shaming a woman for her real or presumed sexual activity, or for behaving in ways that someone thinks are associated with her real or presumed sexual activity.

**Sperm:** The male reproductive cell, consisting of a head, midpiece, and tail. The head contains the genetic material, while the tail is used to propel the sperm as it travels towards the egg.

**Spontaneous Erection:** A penile erection that occurs as an automatic response to a variety of stimuli, some of which is sexual and some of which is physiological.

**STD:** An abbreviation that refers to sexually transmitted diseases. These are illnesses that are communicable through sexual behaviors, including intercourse. Some of these illnesses can also be transmitted through blood contact.

**STI:** An abbreviation that refers to sexually transmitted infections. These are illnesses that are communicable through sexual behaviors, including intercourse. Some of these illnesses can also be transmitted through blood contact. Not all STI's lead to a disease and become an STD.

**Straight:** A slang term for heterosexuality, a sexual orientation in which one is attracted to members of the opposite sex (males are attracted to females; females are attracted to males).

**Syphilis:** A chronic, contagious, usually venereal and often congenital, disease caused by a spirochete, and if left untreated, producing chancres, rashes, and systemic lesions in a clinical course with three stages continued over many years.

**Test Touch:** Seemingly innocent touches by a predator or offender, such as a pat on the back or a squeeze on the arm, that are meant to normalize kids to being in physical contact with the predator. Test touches can progress to trying to be alone with the child.

**Testicles:** The male gonad, which is located inside the scrotum beneath the penis. The testicles are responsible for the production of sperm and androgens, primarily testosterone.

**Transgender:** A condition or state in which one's physical sex does not match one's gender identity. A transgender individual may have been assigned a sex at birth based on their genitals, but feel that this assignation is false or incomplete. They also may be someone who does not conform to conventional gender roles but instead combines or moves between them.

**Uncomfortable:** Feeling or causing discomfort or unease; disquieting.

**Under the Influence:** Being physically affected by alcohol or drugs

**Urethra:** The tube that connects the urinary bladder to the urinary meatus (the orifice through which the urine exits the urethra tube). In males, the urethra runs down the penis and opens at the end of the penis. In females, the urethra is internal and opens between the clitoris and the vagina.

**Urination:** The process through which urine is released from the urinary bladder to travel down the urethra and exit the body at the urinary meatus.

**Uterus:** A major reproductive sex organ in the female body. The uterus is located in the lower half of the torso, just above the vagina. It is the site in which offspring are conceived and in which they gestate during the term of the pregnancy.

**Vagina:** The muscular tube leading from the external genitals to the cervix of the uterus in women. During sexual intercourse, the penis can be inserted into the vagina. During childbirth, the infant exits the uterus through the vagina.

**Vaginal Sex:** A form of sexual intercourse in which the penis is inserted into the vagina.

**Vaginismus:** A medical condition in which a woman is unable to engage in any form of vaginal penetration, including sexual intercourse, the use of tampons or menstrual cups, and  that of gynecological examinations, due to involuntary pain.

**Victim:** A person who is harmed, injured, or killed as the result of an accident or crime.

**Virgin:** A male or female who has never engaged in sexual intercourse.

**Vulva:** The parts of the female sexual organs that are on the outside of the body.

**Wet Dreams :** A slang term for nocturnal emissions. A nocturnal emission is a spontaneous orgasm that occurs during sleep. Nocturnal emissions can occur in both males (ejaculation) and females (lubrication of the vagina).

Made in the USA
Middletown, DE
14 October 2021

50185221R00084